WHAT PEOPLE ARE SAYING ABOUT THE
Sex & Lies Series

It is well past time for Christian people to take their heads out of the proverbial sand and take a hard look at the fare offered to our children and young people through various media outlets and how it affects them. Eva Marie and Jessica Everson's book does just that and should be required reading for every parent, grandparent, and anyone who has a heart for our children and youth in today's sex-saturated culture.
 —DONALD E. WILDMON, CHAIRMAN, AMERICAN FAMILY ASSOCIATION

Eva Marie and Jessica Everson's book Sex, Lies, and the Media *is a readable, much-needed overview of the cultural snares, trials, and temptations that our young people face. Written from the point of view of a concerned mother and her daughter, it is an important, eye-opening building block in the media-wise tools for parents with faith and values. We face a crisis in the mass media of entertainment's brainwashing of our children and grandchildren, and this book is the first step in extricating our children and grandchildren from the clutches of the mass media.*
 —DR. TED BAEHR, CHAIRMAN, CHRISTIAN FILM AND TELEVISION COMMISSION;
 AND PUBLISHER, MOVIEGUIDE

This dynamic mother/daughter duo add an important voice to the national dialogue on sex and the media. Their thoughtful and well-thought-out words allow us all to take a deep breath on the subject and evaluate what course of action we wish to take. This book reminds us that we are all susceptible to believing false images and ideals. It challenges us to look inside, dig deeper, and never, never stop talking to our children about this issue.
 —JESSICA WEINER, AUTHOR, *A VERY HUNGRY GIRL: HOW I FILLED UP
 ON LIFE AND HOW YOU CAN, TOO!*

This book should be required reading for every parent of a teenager. Eva Marie and Jessica Everson have done a fabulous job of unveiling the damaging influences of the media. Parents are left without excuse—they have done the homework for us.
 —VICKI COURTNEY, FOUNDER, VIRTUOUS REALITY; NATIONAL SPEAKER; AND BEST-SELLING
 AUTHOR, *YOUR GIRL: RAISING A GODLY DAUGHTER IN AN UNGODLY WORLD*

In this no-nonsense guide for parents, Eva Marie and Jessica Everson equip parents with the tools to understand the forces in our culture that negatively influence the next generation—and offer practical suggestions on how to deal with them. Well-researched and to-the-point, this book will be a handy reference for parents who want to understand the world of their kids.
 —STEVEN JAMES, POPULAR CONFERENCE SPEAKER AND AUTHOR OF THE TEEN
 DEVOTIONALS *HOW TO SMELL LIKE GOD* AND *PRAYING FROM THE GUT*

This is a landmark book for parenting in the twenty-first century and represents a major contribution to moral excellence in rearing children to successful emancipation. My thinking was reordered as I read this manuscript, and I marked page after page of important safeguards necessary to raise pure kids in an impure world. Astonished, informed, encouraged, equipped ... these are the buzzwords that will be swirling around this deeply vital book.

—RENEE DURFIELD, DD, AUTHOR, *RAISING PURE KIDS IN AN IMPURE WORLD;* EXECUTIVE DIRECTOR, FOR WEDLOCK ONLY

Eva Marie and Jessica Everson address the much needed topic of how to navigate the waters of media and popular culture. The findings of this well-researched book may well shock some Christians who've had their heads comfortably buried in the sand. Our kids—not just "those other" kids, but even Christian kids—are not only surrounded by, but are also imitating the sexual permissiveness that they're watching in films and TV and hearing in their music. So what's a parent to do? The Eversons first open our eyes, then offer some practical helps. As an actress myself for the past twenty years, I especially appreciated their point of view: They didn't simply condemn media as a whole, nor do they ignore the reality of its presence and impact on our lives. Instead, with biblical insights and practical suggestions, they re-empower parents to be parents. And part of that responsibility is to teach children to become wise consumers of the media they watch and the music they listen to. This is a book that every family needs to read.

—NANCY STAFFORD, ACTRESS, *MATLOCK;* SPEAKER; AND AUTHOR, *THE WONDER OF HIS LOVE: A JOURNEY INTO THE HEART OF GOD* AND *BEAUTY BY THE BOOK: SEEING YOURSELF AS GOD SEES YOU*

A "no apologies" and "in-your-face" Christian response to the in-your-face affront of the secular media in the lives of our children. Eva Marie and Jessica Everson tell it like it is so we as parents can tell it like it is to our kids.

—VICKI CARUANA, AMERICA'S TEACHER, AUTHOR OF THE BEST-SELLING BOOK *APPLES AND CHALKDUST* AND *GIVING YOUR CHILD THE EXCELLENCE EDGE*

Years ago as a teen mom, I made devastating choices that changed the course of my life. I bought into the worldly lies of sex, drugs, and rock 'n' roll, filling the empty places in my heart and soul with even emptier promises and pursuits. My life changed when I made my U-turn toward God. Eva Marie and Jessica Everson tell it like it is in this powerful and eye-opening must-read, giving today's parents and teens a chance to make life-changing U-turns of their own—based on truth.

—ALLISON BOTTKE, SPEAKER AND AUTHOR, *GOD ALLOWS U-TURNS*

Eva Marie and Jessica Everson's book gives discouraging facts with positive suggestions. I believe this book will be a valuable resource for both parents and youth workers.

—JAMES LI (JAMES SANG LEE), YOUTH MINISTRIES DIRECTOR, NORTHLAND: A CHURCH DISTRIBUTED; MARTIAL ARTS CHAMPION; AND MOVIE STUNTMAN

For parents crying for help against the intrusion of media, Sex, Lies, and the Media *answers their pleas. For parents who aren't aware of the snares of media,* Sex, Lies, and the Media *opens their eyes. This "nothing-held-back" look at today's world, arms all parents with the weaponry needed to win the battle for the souls of their children.*

—JILL RIGBY, AUTHOR, *RAISING RESPECTFUL CHILDREN IN A DISRESPECTFUL WORLD;* PRESIDENT AND CEO, MANNERS OF THE HEART COMMUNITY FUND

Eva Marie Everson
Jessica Everson

LIFE JOURNEY®
Bringing Home the Message for Life

COOK COMMUNICATIONS MINISTRIES
Colorado Springs, Colorado • Paris, Ontario
KINGSWAY COMMUNICATIONS LTD
Eastbourne, England

Life Journey® is an imprint of
Cook Communications Ministries, Colorado Springs, CO 80918
Cook Communications, Paris, Ontario
Kingsway Communications, Eastbourne, England

SEX, LIES, AND HIGH SCHOOL

Published in association with the literary agency of The Knight Agency, 577 South
Main St., Madison, GA 30650.

The Web site addresses (URLs) recommended throughout this book are solely
offered as a resource to the reader. The citation of these Web sites does not in any
way imply an endorsement on the part of the authors or the publisher, nor do the
authors or publisher vouch for their content for the life of this book.

Cover Design: BMB Design
First Printing, 2006

Printed in the United States of America

10 9 8 7 6 5 4 3 2 1 Printing/Year 10 09 08 07 06

ISBN-13: 978-0-7814-4359-3
ISBN-10: 0-7814-4359-8

LCCN: 2006928058

Eva Marie
dedicates this book to her niece,
Lisa Walraven,
Class of 2005,
because she got through it all ... and so beautifully!
You go, girl!

Jessica Everson
dedicates this book
To PaPa
Who taught me to "Keep on keeping on...."

Contents

Foreword

Imagine you're canoeing down a river. Up ahead, just around the next bend, you hear rapids. You know what's coming. Your heart starts jack-hammering in your chest. You grip your paddle more tightly and curl it through the water.

You feel the tug of the current.

The pull reminds you of the last time you were on this river, years ago. Sometimes it seems like a whole lifetime ago. Sure, you made it through. But it wasn't easy. You made some mistakes that have cost you over the years. And since then, the river has become even more dangerous. The current flows faster now than it ever has in history.

The water swirls around your canoe, picking up speed.

These rapids can be deadly. Most people don't make it through them unscathed. Some people have never even made it past this section of the river. And today you're even more nervous because someone else rides in the canoe with you; up in the front. You can help steer a little, but you don't get to choose the course down the river. That's up the person in the front of the boat.

That's up to your teenager.

"Let's pull over to shore and scout out the rapids!" you shout over the roar of the river. The person in the front nods and you head to shore.

After tying your boat to a tree, you walk up the shore. "See that eddy over there, where the river is calm?" you ask. Your son or daughter nods. "We can rest there. And there's a waterfall over there on left side of the river, we need to avoid that."

From the shore you can step back, take the time to look at what lies beyond the next bend, and plan how you're going to maneuver through the rapids. You can show your teen what to avoid and where to aim the boat of their lives.

In this book Eva Marie and Jessica, seasoned river guides, take us to shore and show us how to help our sons and daughters maneuver through the rapids of adolescence strewn with the swift currents and cataracts of teen fashion, crushes, spring break, prom, and dating—choices that will influence them for the rest of their lives.

After all, one of the major rapids teens must navigate today is sexual temptation. According to the American Academy of Child and Adolescent Psychiatry, each year about one million teenage girls become pregnant in the United States and three million teens get a sexually transmitted disease. In our culture, youth are exposed to sexual images and messages on a daily, sometimes hourly, basis. The current is swift and the rapids can be brutal.

This book offers the chance to step away from the rush and swirl of everyday life and see how you can help your children maneuver successfully through the next few years—how to make it past the rapids without capsizing.

Of course, your job isn't to paddle for your children. They're choosing. They're deciding. But you can show them how to make it through. You can help steer them in the right direction with encouragement, guidance, and Christ-like love.

This book will show you how.

Steven James
Conference speaker and author of *Praying From the Gut: An Honest Prayer Journal for Teens* and *How to Smell Like God: Spiritual Aromatherapy for Teens*

Introduction

Or, Were These Really the Best of Times?

S omewhere in the dusty, musty cabinets of an antique sideboard are six old high school yearbooks. My husband's range over a three-year period during the 1960s. Mine cover a three-year period during the 1970s. Periodically, I pull them out, wipe away the dust, and crack open the covers. Turning the glossy pages, I take in the photos of friends I swore I'd never forget but can now barely remember. Fortunately, a few of them had scribbled words of affection nearby, saying things like:

> Roses are red
> Violets are blue
> Never forget me and
> I'll never forget you!

If only it were that simple.

Like many in my graduating class, I left my hometown as soon I was done with high school. Let me rephrase that. I *ran* from my hometown.

Now, as I peer down at the *Panorama*'s slick pages of black-and-white photographs and written mementos, I pause to remember *why*. It doesn't take long, though. Those years, like the years described in

Dickens's classic *A Tale of Two Cities*, were truly "the best of times ... the worst of times."

What most adults remember twenty-five or thirty years later are the good times: days filled with laughter, music, and passing notes to friends as we crossed paths in the hallways between classes. We remember innocent pranks, favorite teachers, and local hangouts. We recall first dates, movies at the drive-in (or the movie theater, if your town had one), and dancing cheek-to-cheek under the mirrored ball at the prom. We think back on the one-act plays performed by the drama department, state science fairs, ball games, and on-the-road sports tournaments and band competitions. We chuckle as we recall the class clown and the hilarity of "Pajama Day." And if we think long enough and hard enough, we might even remember opening books, reading them, learning from them, and taking pop quizzes, which always left us baffled by their unexpectedness.

Yes, those were the "best of times."

But we have to be honest, don't we? We also remember our bodies working against us: trying so hard to keep our faces scrubbed and fresh, only to have those nasty little zits pop out at the most inopportune times and in the most obvious places; staying on top of fashion's whims—and thereby being cool—was nearly a full-time job. On Monday we were tired, on Wednesday we were ready to rock and roll, and by Friday we were in a panic if we didn't have a date for Saturday night.

If we had a "steady," we had a whole new set of problems. To "do it" or *not* to "do it," that was the question. *How far is too far?* burned a question mark in our brains. Our hormones raged whether we had a steady or not, and we struggled with a million reasons to "go all the way" and a million and one to stay pure.

Those who made church and youth group a weekly part of our lives struggled all the more. If we'd pressed against the restraints of boundary on Saturday night, we were doubly doomed when we sat in God's presence on Sunday. *Can the pastor see to the deepest parts of my soul? Was that a smirk on the face of Mrs. Prickly, the organist? Can God possibly love a sinner like me? Is this what Paul meant when he wrote, "I do not understand what I do. For what I want to do I do not do, but what I hate I do," and "What a wretched man I am! Who will rescue me from this body of death?"* (Rom. 7:15, 24).

Adding to the mix, of course, were the temptations of drugs and alcohol. The mantra of the 1960s was "Sex, Drugs, and Rock 'n' Roll." This was only a problem *after* school hours. I distinctly remember seeing the glassy eyes of schoolmates as I entered the hallowed halls of high school and refraining from too many trips to the girl's restroom lest the police—who were constantly being called due to racial unrest—decide at *that* moment to raid the place, and I be carted off to jail stone-cold sober, but with my pants down (so to speak). My days consisted of being worried about a permanent scar on my record or waiting until I got home.

Hard times. Difficult choices. Complex years.

And then … they were over. For some of us, mistakes made during high school continued to have consequences long after we were gone. For others, the morning after graduation truly marked the first day of the rest of our lives. Either way, if life made little sense *then,* it made even less sense *after.* We quickly learned adulthood doesn't come with any guarantees of intelligence, but hopefully it brings wisdom.

As parents and grandparents, we understand those struggles a wee bit better. Like *why* we struggled so with our hormones and *what* can happen during spring break and *how* one dance called *prom* can alter the course of our lives. Above all, we see the truths we couldn't have known then and the danger of the lies we once believed. We see youth and sexuality in a different light.

And many of us wish we could go back and just do it all over again. This time we'd get it right. *Wouldn't we?*

This book is for parents, grandparents, or guardians of teens either already in high school or about to enter its world. We undertook hours of research in preparing *Sex, Lies, and High School*, our way of making it easier for you to know what's happening in the daily, sex-saturated life of your child. Whether your child is sexually active or not, he or she is inundated with sexually explicit, confusing messages. We hope the information contained within these pages will help you help your teen make positive, godly decisions.

> I was having a discussion with my fourteen-year-old son recently regarding sex, porn, etc. ... During the course of our chat he said something that I thought profound for a young man of his age. He said, "Mom, it's like my generation is growing up in dog years." I couldn't help but smile and feel sad at the same time. Wow, is he seeing the truth through the fog!"[2]
>
> —Carolyn Ruch, mother

This is the second book on which I've collaborated with my daughter Jessica. I can only tell you what I've recently read and researched. Jessica can tell you what she's recently lived through. She'll also be the first one to tell you that even in the short period of time since she graduated from high school, things have changed drastically; that they will continue to change; that they will get worse. So read Jessica's words carefully.

High school doesn't have to be the worst of times for your child—if you'll read this book, talk to your child, and above all, pray.

This is the truth about sex, lies, and high school.

—Eva Marie Everson

HOW TO READ THIS BOOK

Our suggestion for reading this book is to take it one step at a time. It contains a lot of information and statistics that can become overwhelming. (Even writing it was a bit much at times.) We tried to be honest and revealing about both what we know from books and, more important, what we've lived through.

You'll also find paragraphs in each chapter labeled "Jessica's Blog." Within these paragraphs you'll read Jessica's heartfelt candor about today's youth and their complex world. You will also read sections of questions asked of experts—mostly high school students and recent graduates. The answers—though they may stun you from time to time—are key to understanding the hearts and minds of today's youth.

Our final suggestion is to read this book *with* someone. Your child's other parent, for example, or grandparents. If you are a single parent, read the book along with another or other single parents. Form a reading group and—armed with this information—determine what you can do to make the high school years of your children the best they can be.

If you work with teens, read the book with others within your community who do the same. Again, talk about what you can do within the context of your role to help make these years better—years your teens won't look back on with regret.

CHAPTER 1

Sex, Lies, and the Teen Years

Or, Getting to Know Them

Teenagers don't come with an instruction manual—life would sure be easier if they did!

> —JILL SAVAGE AND PAM FARREL, *GOT TEENS?*

The other day our seven-year-old granddaughter asked permission to have our little next-door neighbor over for a tea party, which would be held in the bedroom she has in our house. Permission granted, she ran next door to ask if her friend could join her. Minutes later, I watched the two girls, ages seven and five, come running back down the sidewalk with our neighbor's youngest child—a boy, age four—not far behind.

As soon as they came under the covering of the front porch, I heard my granddaughter say, "You can't come to the tea party, Billy!" (The inflection was something akin to "duh!")

"Why not?" Billy asked.

"Tea parties are for girls, Billy," she answered.

I opened the door to see how I might help out. "Billy," I said, "the girls will have a tea party in Jordynn's room. And we don't let little boys come into the bedrooms of little girls."

Well, Billy cried. Cried and ran all the way back home, breaking my heart and confusing my granddaughter. "Why would he want to be at a girl's tea party?" she asked my husband and me later. "I didn't want to hurt his feelings."

"Well," my husband began, slow and full of wisdom. "You see, right now Billy is at an age where he won't mind playing girl games with you in your bedroom. But give him a couple of years, and he wouldn't be caught dead in your bedroom." Then my husband rolled his eyes. "A few years after that, and he'll be trying to get back in again," he said under his breath.

"And he won't be allowed in then, either," I added, stroking her hair. Then I looked to my husband. "Oh, how little you boys change," I said with a smile.

Who Are You and What Have You Done with My Baby?

In his book, *The Teen Health Book: A Parents' Guide to Adolescent Health and Well-Being*, Dr. Ralph I. Lopez writes: "No one entertaining the idea of having a baby imagines the pleasures of having a teenager."[1]

Something tells me there was a bit of sarcasm in the word *pleasures*.

Not that teens can't be a fount of many blessings, but have you ever felt as though you went to bed one night only to get up the next morning to discover some alien life form had broken into your home in the middle of the night, abducted your precious angel, and left a monster in his or her place?

When did the eye-rolling start? The heavy sighing? Where does all the anger come from, and what do they mean when they say, "My pants are too short," or "My shoes are too small," or "This blouse won't button anymore"? Didn't you just buy all those things? How can a child grow so much, and overnight at that?

Physically, it can happen overnight. Or at least at night. It's during our sons' and daughters' sleeping hours that growth hormones are released. In fact, the release of the hormone responsible for initiating puberty (the period of time when children begin to mature biologically, psychologically, socially, and cognitively[2]) is sleep-dependent. That said, one could easily see why sleep is of vital importance to a teen and pre-teen. And yet, their sleep patterns are wishy-washy. In studies, nearly half of teens reported at least occasional difficulty falling or staying asleep.[3]

What are the results? Bad moods we parents liken to an attack from the enemy camp; behavior that swings on a pendulum; poor academic performance; depression; a greater risk of negative self-image.

Adolescence (the transitional period between childhood and adulthood[4]) and the changes it brings don't begin the day kids walk into high school. Between the ages of eleven and fourteen (early adolescence), children undergo a multitude of physical, emotional, and spiritual changes that will affect them later on. During those increasingly turbulent high school years, when everything rides on a teeter-totter foundation and peer pressure, teens bounce back and forth from dependence ("Mom! Dad! I need you!") to independence ("Ohmygosh! What are you *doing*? I can handle this!"). They go from letting you in on their deepest secrets to telling you nothing at all.

These are the years that take much prayer and fortitude to get through. And years later, when you hold the baby of your baby in your arms, these are the years of which you'll say, "I'm glad I let you live."

BOYS AND GIRLS

The brain knows when the body is nearing sexual maturity and, in turn, releases chemicals called hormones. Different hormones are responsible for different changes. As your teen child—whether your son or daughter—draws nearer to puberty, the brain and pituitary gland release hormones that regulate the reproductive organs. They'll stimulate the ovaries of your daughters to produce other hormones called estrogen and progesterone, and they'll stimulate the testes of your sons to produce testosterone.

BOYS

With the production of hormones in adolescence (between the ages of ten and eighteen), your son will go through a variety of changes.

Physically, the most obvious changes will be that his feet and hands begin to grow, his shoulders become wider, and he becomes more muscular. His voice will change, growing deeper, and perhaps squeaking a bit along the way. Hair begins to sprout on his face, under his arms, and around his genitals, which will begin to enlarge and darken. By fifteen a tiny tangle of tubes (miniature factories that turn out sperm on a massive scale—a thousand every second[5]) will have grown inside the testicles. Nocturnal emissions—also known as wet dreams, the uncontrolled ejaculation of semen from the penis during sleep—will occur somewhere between the ages of twelve and eighteen. Wet dreams are normal and healthy, caused by such variants as the bed, a blanket or sheet causing physical stimulation, a dream, or a full bladder. They are also a sign that your son is beginning to move toward sexual maturity, but you can relax in the knowledge that sexual maturity is not sexual activity.

> Bras are less a rite of passage, because they have become fashion accessories.[6]
>
> —Dr. Ralph I. Lopez

During the time of adolescence, visual stimulation reminds a young man that his penis has a mind of its own. But physical changes and desires are not the only changes to boys at this time. Young boys-to-men also find themselves desiring emotional fulfillment as well. However, they're not yet adults.

Girls

It takes four years for a girl to be fully transformed into an adult. This transformation can begin anywhere from age eight to thirteen. Unlike their male counterparts whose bodies become more muscular, girls get curvy, developing a little more fat on their hips. Overall they begin to add body fat. As long as the body fat does not lean toward obesity, this is a good thing because, for a girl, puberty is brought on by fat and is necessary for her menstrual cycle to begin.

Hair, underarm and pubic, begins to grow. Breasts begin to bud and develop. If they grow too large, unwanted attention may be showered upon your daughter—attention she may not be ready to handle. If they don't seem to grow fast enough, your daughter may feel as though she's not keeping up with her peers or that she has to prove her sexuality in other ways. Or, feeling the pressure, she may ask for breast augmentation. More than 150,000 women had breast augmentation surgery last year, an all-time high. And the number of teenagers who chose breast implants more than doubled in the last two years.[7]

All these changes in a young girl have one primary physiological purpose: to make babies.

CONTROL

All these physical changes are issues neither you nor your child has control over. At some point, your son and daughter will leave a child body behind and begin heading toward an adult body, and there is nothing you can do to stop it. By the time they hit high school, they should be well on their way.

But the attitudes and feelings from these external changes are things they *can* control—at least to a degree. You can help by providing your child with a sense that you are okay with talking about the changes and about their sexuality in general.

Yes, Mommy and Daddy—or by this point Mom and Dad—your child has a sexuality. Teens are *sexual beings*. They have been perfected and formed by their loving Creator to undergo all these frightening and exciting changes and to have all the feelings associated with them. Let them (and yourself!) know it really is okay. But remember: Just because they are sexual doesn't mean they *have to have* or *are having* sex.

Dr. Ralph I. Lopez writes in his book *The Teen Health Book; A Parents' Guide to Adolescent Health and Well-Being,* that there are three questions adolescents must answer as they pass from childhood to adulthood:

WHO AM I?

During the teen years children begin to explore their own beliefs versus yours, from politics to religion and everything in between. You may like contemporary Christian music, the sound of the '80s, or even soft rock and roll, but your children will begin to make their own choices about music and other forms of entertainment.

JESSICA'S BLOG

This means they will begin to challenge ideas and institutions, maybe even values you hold dear. They will also challenge (at least to themselves if not also among their friends and even their parents) beliefs on abstinence and sex as a "wedding gift" from God. They will begin to think about things like: When is the right time for me? What will the first time be like? What are my friends doing? They'll even have questions about what sex really is and at what point a person truly loses their virginity.

WHO AM I SEXUALLY?

Don't be horrified if your children feel differently about sex or their sexuality than you think they should feel. It would be a perfect world if they agreed with you, but we don't live in a perfect world. More important, they live in a world in which teens are bombarded by sexual images, suggestions, and encouragements. In one year they will see approximately 14,000 sexual images, with less than 170 of them being positive (such as about birth control, self-control, abstinence, pregnancy, or STDs).[8] And while it's not something we ever want to have to contemplate, your child may struggle with sexual identification and/or preference. If that is the case, there are Christian organizations that can help you.

JESSICA'S BLOG

Naturally, teens are going to be concerned about their part in the world of sex. Their curiosity has them thinking lots of grown-up and somewhat graphic thoughts about such things as how capable they will be, whether they would satisfy someone, shouldn't they practice so they could satisfy someone, and should they experiment more? They also may think: What would it do to my parents if they found out I was having sex? What will they do to me? What will the guy/girl I like do if I don't? And what will my friends say if they find out I'm trying to wait?

HOW DO I BECOME INDEPENDENT?

At some point your teens won't need you to drive them to school, to see their friends, to the mall, or even to church. In fact, they'll prefer that you don't. They'll test boundaries in a variety of ways, including where they go, how late they stay out, and what they do once they get there. They'll withhold information from you—not because they are doing something wrong, but because they are beginning to see themselves as individuals and not as a subunit of their parents.

They are becoming adults, Mom and Dad, and it is *your* job to help in this transformation. We want our little caterpillars to become lovely, magnificent butterflies who float on the air of fulfillment and success, not nocturnal, dull moths that eat away at the clothes of others. Just as a butterfly forms in a chrysalis and should not be released too soon lest it fall to the ground and die, neither should we let go of our sons or daughters too soon.

Set your boundaries, and keep them. Parents must be parents. For now, let their friends be their friends. Your time for unbroken friendship will come soon enough and will last a lifetime.

Remember that rational thinking, for your teens, will not be the norm. But it is important that you understand their insecurities during these years and recognize that they will often feel as if no one understands them.

Jessica's Blog

In our book *Sex, Lies, and the Media,* we stress parents' teachable moments as those moments when media gives us an opportunity to expose some of the lies of popular culture to children. I would like to take this time to insert a new idea. Kids have teachable moments too! These are the moments they give us a glimpse into their world.

> As teenagers undergo the changes of puberty, they have no choice but to see themselves in a sexual light.[9]
>
> —Dr. Ralph I. Lopez

Although adolescent kids are struggling to find their identity and independence, they still want to share some of their new discoveries with you. Try not to miss these opportunities. They are times of bonding. How you handle moments like these will help determine how comfortable your kids will be sharing things with you in the future. Doing things together—fun things—will spark these moments, but you must learn to recognize them. To miss them, even without intending to, will be translated as rejection. And like anyone else, hormone-ridden teens don't like to feel rejection. They will remember this feeling when the subject becomes more serious.

So be open-minded to the things they try to introduce to you. A song, a TV show, an idea, or a story. It could even be in an unexpected, undeserved outburst. Ever gotten one of these from your teen?

You ask a question or make a comment and in response you get something suited for one's worst enemy? Something else is probably on their mind. Try responding sensitively and persistently until you find out what is behind the outburst. It may or may not have anything to do with your previous remarks.

So take a noticeable interest in the things that interest them—even the ones you don't like. You may not like the song, you may not appreciate the tone in their voice, but they're reaching out to you nonetheless. Isn't that what you want?

JESSICA'S Q & A BLOG

NOW YOU TELL ME: WHAT'S IT LIKE TO BE A LARGE-BREASTED TEEN GIRL?

Rebeca (twentysomething, mother of one): I can definitely answer this question. My (large) breasts developed when I was twelve. I got tons of male interest when I didn't even have an idea as to who I was, much less what I wanted in a boy. There was the inability to compete in team sports (running up and down a basketball court can get quite obscene, and it's difficult to find sports bras for big-busted girls).

There was difficulty finding appropriate clothing. Everything that fit my waist was too tight across my breasts. Everything that fit my breasts hung like a sheet on the rest of my body. The assumption by everyone outside of school, friends, and family was that I was older than I really was. When you're young that's *great,* but not so great when a twenty-three-year-old is hitting on you and you're unsure how to act.

There's also the inability to fit in with the other girls. They were all buying cute little padded bras while I was searching for anything that wasn't made completely of white cotton. Then there's posture. In an effort to appear smaller, I walked hunched over.

Self-image is another issue. Large breasts make a girl's entire body look larger. She can begin to think she is overweight when, in actuality, it's her breasts. (I really suffered with this and even got to the point of becoming anorexic. Thankfully, I stayed that way for only a year because I realized I wasn't *fat*, just my breasts were!)

> Treat ... older women as mothers, and younger women as sisters, with absolute purity.
>
> —1 Tim. 5:1–2

Then, of course, there's the prom. Prom dresses are definitely not made for the large-breasted girl. Every one of my prom dresses (I went to five) had to be altered or handmade because of my breasts.

Parents should recognize that, though *they* may have perspective, their daughter doesn't. She is immersed in a world where image reigns supreme and her image doesn't fit the mold. She'll be worried, frustrated, annoyed, and tired of not having her body look like her friends'. Telling her that her outer beauty doesn't matter—that it's all about what's inside—won't help much today. Remind her that beauty comes from individuality. Make her image difference be a positive thing *à la,* "Who would want to look like everyone else? You stand out in a crowd!"

Do your homework to find clothes that will fit her body. *Do not drape her in jackets or clothes that are too big!* This may communicate to her that her breasts are something to be ashamed of. Instead, help her find clothing that is comfortable and appropriate. Take T-shirts to the tailor if you have to so they don't balloon around her waist or stretch tight across her chest.

Finally, draw attention to her other characteristics. If she has lovely eyes, say so. If her hair is gorgeously thick and long, say so. For her, image can become entirely about her chest. By reminding her she has other features, you remind her she has an entire body, not just a huge set of breasts.

How about fathers to sons? How should they teach them about respect, etc., as it deals with this subject?

Fathers, please say to your sons: *Do* not *assume that because a girl has big breasts she is sexually active!* You would not believe how many guys I went out with who assumed I was ready to hop into the backseat because my body looked ready. Ugh, so annoying!

Fathers should remind their sons to look at a girl's face when she's talking (or he's talking to her) rather than at her chest. Teach sons to compliment a girl on any other feature—nice eyes, beautiful outfit, great hair, etc. Teach them that handholding is much better than hugging (or go for the from-the-side hug). The girl has probably been taught not to hug guys because it presses her chest up against him. Even if she hasn't, she has probably learned that hugging can be painful if the guy holds her too tightly. Teach them to put an arm around her waist or hold her hand.

Fathers should explain to their sons that the girl might feel inferior to her peers because of her chest. He can teach his son to build the girl's self esteem by having conversations with her, noting her other features, and being considerate of her.

Finally, no jokes with his buddies about her nice "rack." Even if she never learns of this crass behavior, it serves to belittle her in men's eyes and is therefore cruel.

CHAPTER 2

Sex, Lies, and Heartthrobs

Or, Move Over, Brat Pack

Every generation needs men of courage, men of conviction, men of strength—men of God.

—JOSHUA HARRIS, *NOT EVEN A HINT*

Bobby Sherman. David Cassidy. Peter Tork. Leonard Whiting. What do these four men have in common? They were heartthrobs whose glossy posters graced nearly every square inch of the pale yellow walls in the bedroom of my high school years. Years later, while I was raising kids, it was posters of the likes of Rick Springfield, the Brat Pack, and Tom Cruise that were the most popular.

But heartthrobs didn't begin in my day or even in yours, if you are a parent of one or more of today's teens. Some of the *most* famous teen idols were created in the late 1950s and early 1960s. And I mean *created*.

WHO WAS ELVIS, REALLY?

He has to have been one of the most popular heartthrobs of all time. He certainly—to date—is the best-selling solo artist in U.S. history and had more charted songs on Billboard's Top 100 than any other artist.[1] But Elvis Aaron Presley didn't just slip into a studio one day, sing a song, and become an overnight sensation. He was *made* into one. If we start with number one, maybe we can begin to understand how all those who rose to stardom after him came to be.

In 1953 Elvis walked into a small recording studio, Memphis Recording Service. He recorded a couple of songs at $3.98 a pop and left. The following year, he returned, recorded two more songs, and again walked out the door.

Sam Phillips, who owned both Memphis Recording Service and the independent Sun Records, heard Elvis and—though he was looking for a white man who could sing R&B like a black man—was not impressed with the young mechanic who would eventually turn the music and movie industry upside down.

But a few months later, Elvis reentered the studio to record "That's Alright Mama." This time, Phillips took notice.

By 1955, Elvis had five recordings under his belt and a tad of local popularity. Enter Colonel Tom Parker, a mastermind in marketing. By launching a national-exposure campaign for the young Tennessean, Parker *created* a star. And as we all now know, he also produced a walking time bomb and one of the saddest stories to ever *grace* rock and roll.

> Whatever Elvis's other problems may have been, his biggest failing was his utter dependence upon his manager, Colonel Tom Parker. When they inked their first contract, Parker took an unusual 25 percent commission; by the time of the King's death, three-fourths of Elvis's income went into Parker's pocket, seemingly without Elvis's knowledge. If Elvis was Faust, selling his soul for the riches of the earth, Parker will always be Mephistopheles, paying with a mess of pottage.[2]

TODAY'S IDOLS

In the early days of modern media it was not unusual for motion picture actors to be turned into recording artists and vice versa. Take Frank Sinatra, for example. Now, I know you'll have to think really,

really far back to remember this member of the original Rat Pack. But "Old Blue Eyes" is just one example of "American Idols" who began their rise to fame within one level of entertainment and crossed over to another.

America's youth were screaming hysterically for Frank and Elvis both as music makers and as faces on the big screen. They swooned over Cary Grant and Rock Hudson (movies) and Dion and the Belmonts and the Beatles (music). In the '70s, young girls wanted the fresh scrubbed looks of Cheryl Tiegs—whom *Time* magazine called "The All American Model"[3]—and Cybill Shepherd, who later went on to sing in Las Vegas and star on several hit television shows. The '80s and '90s saw a resurgence of the supermodel with Tyra Banks and Cindy Crawford.

But today it's not the movie and television stars or the leggy models who draw America's youth. While in the '80s soap opera stars were fairly hot, now celebrities like Rick Springfield, John Stamos, and "Luke and Laura"—actors Anthony Geary and Genie Francis—have faded. Today's youth are drawn more toward music artists, no matter the genre. Parents would do well to get to know them at least half as well as their children do.

We've long known that teens with mentors in their lives—admired individuals to whom they can turn for help or advice—demonstrate lower levels of risk-taking behavior such as substance abuse and unprotected sexual activity. The data here, however, represent the first scientific demonstration that role models introduced to teens by the media also exert a positive influence. Despite the highly publicized falls from grace of some athletes and actors, sports and other public figures have a positive influence on the lives of admiring teens.[4]

—Dr. Antronette K. Yancey, lead author and community health sciences professor in the School of Public Health

LET'S NOT FORGET ...

This chapter would not be complete without talking about sports figures. High-profile sports figures rank near the top in their influence over teens, as well. Football, baseball, basketball, soccer, and tennis. Speed skating, figure skating, hockey, snow skiing, and water sports. Motor sports, martial arts, swimming, and track. The list goes on and on.

In 2002 the UCLA School of Public Health issued the findings of a study performed on 750 Los Angeles County teens, giving the first scientific evidence that sports stars have a positive influence in the lives of our young people.[5]

A study published in the January 2002 edition of *Archives of Pediatrics and Adolescent Medicine* noted that 56 percent of teens surveyed said they had role models in their lives. The most popular were parents at 22 percent, followed by sports figures at 18 percent. Boys were more likely to list sports stars and other public figures, and girls were more likely to name known individuals.

Interestingly, the study showed that teens who named these role models earned higher grades, had higher levels of self-esteem and stronger ethnic identity than those who said they had no role models.

While *any* media role model can give teens a sense of hard work and accomplishment, sports figures tend to do this to a higher degree. Through sports we see the results of physical discipline and dedication as well as learning the benefits of working within the framework of a team. But we also know those who climb the sports success ladder have an even higher potential of slipping down the rungs. We hear of drug usage, unusual sexual practices, adultery and other out-of-marriage sexual escapades, and of social and civil laws being broken. We also see these young men and women using their sexuality to sell products and, in turn, to make money.

How then should we respond to our children when their favorite hero falls from grace? By way of honesty, remind your children of the human frailty of the man or woman. Tell them this does not eliminate the *results* of the hard work, though it can drastically change the end of a career. If your child is actively involved in a sport—whether the same sport or a similar sport—continue to encourage her to press toward her goal. *The goal has not changed!*

Ask your children, "If you were to achieve equal status in a sport, how do you think you could avoid the same pitfall?" Then remind them of the difference they can make in the sports world by being successful both in sport and in life. And point to the figures—both Christian and secular—who have remained faithful to God and/or to the sport.

So What Are They Looking For?

Have you ever wondered why teens and preteens are so drawn to men and women they don't even know? Why they would look up to, listen to, watch, or observe people like Frank Sinatra, Bobby Sherman, R. Kelly, Jessica Simpson, Britney Spears, and Eminem?

In an interview for our book *Sex, Lies, and the Media*, Jessica was asked about the importance of parents' roles in the lives of their children. Jessica said something that made my heart beat proudly and my brow shoot straight up. "Kids are going to listen to *somebody*. They'll get their answers from *somewhere*," she said to the interviewer. "Make sure it's you."

Yep. Kids are looking for answers to their questions. They are looking for someone to imitate. The idea of fame and fortune, of fans screaming and reaching at every turn, of hotel suites, and of being escorted from airport to airport seems like a wonderful existence. Those who are called "idols" or "heartthrobs" are rarely photographed when they are crying, lonely, sad, emotionally spent, or spiritually dead. We don't see them being interviewed, being asked questions like "So how does it feel to be pregnant again, by yet another man?" or "When was the last time you *really* loved the one you were with?"

The fact is, what your children see as a glamorous life isn't all it's cracked up to be.

A MODEL'S LIFE

When it comes to supermodels, teens are drawn to them for different reasons. Boys are drawn to seeing them scantily clad in bikinis, spread across the glossy pages of magazines like *Sports Illustrated* or *Maxim*. Girls just want to *be* them. Or, at the least, have their bodies. What they are unaware of is 1) what it takes to look like that and 2) those models rarely actually look like that. They are powdered, puffed, coiffed, and then airbrushed. (Jessica and I were once airbrushed in a photo. It can truly be a wonderful thing; but believe me, it's not reality.)

If your teen is drawn to the life of a supermodel, consider sharing with her Tonya's story. At age fifteen, Tonya Ruiz (a friend of mine) began her modeling career. After being discovered by Eileen Ford and with the blessings of her parents, then sixteen-year-old Tonya left the safety and security of home for Paris. For two years, she traveled the globe and saw her image on magazine covers, posters, billboards, and in commercials and movies.

She saw the best—*and the worst*—the fashion world had to offer. Alongside the fun of photo shoots and travel to exotic locations came rich playboys, alcohol, drugs, and eating disorders. In 1981, feeling desperate, alone, and without hope, she decided to end her life. God, on the other hand, saw a loveliness no photographer could ever capture on film. Because of his love and goodness, he turned her sadness into joy and her ashes into beauty. Tonya traded in her life of modeling and became a pastor's wife, homeschooling mom, author, and speaker. Today she is a grandmother, and she speaks to women—both young and old—about *true beauty*.[6]

A TEACHABLE MOMENT COMPLIMENTS OF BRITNEY

One of the saddest, most heart-wrenching videos I've seen in all my research of currently popular musical artists is Britney Spears' "Everytime." The video begins with a wide sweep of Las Vegas, showing the Palms Hotel, then a close-up of the marquee in front, which has in bright neon letters *Britney Spears, Las Vegas*. There is a bigger-than-life image of Britney's face, though she looks remarkably like Madonna doing her own impersonation of Marilyn Monroe. The sexuality oozes and a leather strap—ironically—has her bound, one end wrapping around one wrist, the other end wrapping around the other wrist.

Enter a stretch limo with fans running toward it and paparazzi cameras flashing. Inside the limo are Britney and a young man, apparently her boyfriend. Neither looks happy. They are far apart from each other on the leather seat and are staring out separate windows. The boyfriend is on his cell phone, and when Britney attempts to touch him, he pushes her away. But when they step out of the car, hands bombard her. Everyone wants a piece of her. "Notice me," she sings. "Take my hand."

> God, our sex is so good ... I've had sex three times today ... he's sweet; I like him.[7]
>
> —Britney Spears, speaking of her then boyfriend Kevin Federline (At the time, Federline was the father of one child, whose mother was due to give birth shortly thereafter to their second child. Britney and Federline married shortly after.)

Throughout the song and video, we see a lonely Britney in a loveless relationship, fighting against the Rag-Mags, being hauled by security guards out of harm's way. We also see her suicide attempt (at least I'm assuming that's what it is when one deliberately slips under the water of one's bath) and her "out of body" experience that takes place in the hospital just as a baby girl is being born in the next room. We see her boyfriend's change of attitude as he jumps into the bathtub in an attempt to pull her out from beneath the velvety smoothness of the water and save her life. And we see the flashbulbs continue to explode as reporters scramble to get her story even in her darkest hour.

I'm not a Britney fan. Most of her videos are extremely sexual and offensive to me as a Christian. But this video left me shaken. I cried. Literally cried. It seems to me that, for once, she was real. She showed the reality behind the glitz and the glamour. And seeing that glimpse, my heart bleeds for her. Jesus literally *bled and died* for her! I sincerely pray for her and suggest you do the same.

TELLING YOUR TEENS THE TRUTH ABOUT IDOLS AND SUCH

My good friend Sandy Austin, a one-time high school phys ed teacher and now the president of the Colorado School Counselor Association and a guidance counselor, tells the following story:

> When I was a high school volleyball coach, it was a huge ordeal picking warm-up songs to play before our matches. Each year the girls invariably wanted to include a song that had sexual innuendo. When I would say no, it always took awhile for me to explain that I didn't want anything playing over the loud-speaker that degraded or demeaned them in any way. At first they would complain, but when I would read the lyrics to them word-for-word, their eyes would be opened, and they would understand my concern.
>
> This is not just happening to this generation. I recently heard a 1970s song that I had liked when I was in high school. As I was singing along with this song playing on an oldies radio station, I became shocked at the sexual innuendo—I had never recognized it before. I don't know if many people stop to think about it.

Before you say one word to your kids about heartthrobs and idols, before you talk to them about the people whose glossy images cover the posters in their rooms or appear in their magazines or on the covers of their CDs, remember your own youth. Remember the guys and gals you once thought were so hot or so cool or so sweet or so b*tchin' you could hardly make it through the day without thinking of them, dreaming of them, wondering what life with them would be like.

Remember this: In *our* day, we were pretty much shielded from the true lives of media's princes and princesses. Time and again, I've heard nostalgic pop stars laugh as they look at an old magazine cover in which details about their lives are exploited, only to say, "That was news to me!" In intimate portrait television shows we learn how a movie star's (or singing sensation's) sexual preferences or habits were carefully hidden because the American public wouldn't understand.

But today! Today the sexual preferences and habits are used to entice fans and audiences. Today sexual preferences and habits are used to *sell.* It's all part of the game.

The athlete that impresses me the most is Allen Iverson of the Philadelphia 76ers. He takes professional basketball to another level. His quickness and agility cannot be matched by any other athlete. He is only six feet tall. He plays among giants and still cannot be contained. He scores by will and makes his teammates look better. But, he has a bit of a thug image. People think he is a bad person because he is covered in tattoos and cornrows his hair. Well, I think society bases a little too much on image as it is. Iverson is an African American. Many kids that look up to him are African American. They don't judge him because he is black, or because he has tattoos and wears do-rags. These kids look up to him for one reason: he can play basketball.[8]

—Justin, age eighteen, Kentucky

Before we hear from some savvy teens and those who work with them, let's see how the strange lives and loves of the stars can turn into teachable moments. We'll use a music artist as an example, because of the influence they have today. Consider the brilliant singer, songwriter, and producer R. Kelly. If you are unfamiliar with R. Kelly, I promise you, you know his songs, "I Believe I Can Fly" and "If I Could Turn Back the Hands of Time."

So let's say your child tells you he or she absolutely *loves* the music of R. Kelly. Aspires even to produce, sing, or write like R. Kelly. Now's your turn for a teachable moment. If you don't already know the details of R. Kelly's life and career, go to the Internet and surf yourself silly! It took me less than three minutes to find the following:

Robert Kelly was born January 8, 1969, in Chicago. At the age of twenty-five, R. Kelly married fifteen-year-old Aaliyah, whose album he'd produced earlier that year. The marriage was later annulled and Aaliyah, who never admitted to the marriage, became an acting and singing star, but tragically died in a plane crash in August 2001.

Some of Kelly's song titles include: "Sex Me," "Bump n' Grind," "Your Body's Callin'," and "Feelin' on Yo Booty."[10]

In 2002, twenty-year-old Patrice Jones filed a suit against Kelly for alleged statutory rape four years earlier and for forcing her to have an abortion. A month later, Kelly was arrested for twenty-one counts of child pornography, including possession of a videotape in which he had sex with a fourteen-year-old girl. A month after this, Kelly was sued for videotaping a private moment in the singer's bed. The tape has since landed just about everywhere. In January 2003, Kelly was again arrested on additional charges of child porn.[9]

Armed with this information, what can you do? First, remember that kids know exactly what they are watching and listening to. Don't let them tell you they don't. They do. If they are drawn to a certain type of music or a particular movie star, it's for a reason. In many ways they are saying, "Now, you! *You* understand me!"

Next, discover what it is about the image that attracts your child. Is it the *way* they play the music? "I like this way his fingers move on the piano or how he holds the drumsticks" for example. Is your child musical? Does he also like to make music? Then encourage him to continue to do so, but draw him to more positive role models, such as Switchfoot; Relient K; Third Day; Mary, Mary; Toby Mac; Thousand Foot Krutch; or the Afters, to name but a few. If you have any difficulty with this, click on www.youthfire.com/media/compare/, where you'll find a section titled: "If you like this secular artist, try *this* Christian artist." You also could take a little trip to your local Christian Store and have a conversation with the person in charge of music, read *CCM Magazine,* do further research on the Internet, or talk to the youth pastor at your church.

> "For I know the plans I have for you," declares the LORD, "plans to prosper you and not to harm you, plans to give you hope and a future."
>
> —Jeremiah 29:11

Don't tear down the artist, no matter what they're doing or what they've done. I did something like this one time in jest and, quite frankly, thought nothing of it. Later my daughter came to me and told me how offended she was that *as a Christian I would be so judgmental of another human life.* I apologized, saying, "You're right. While I can say the action or actions are wrong, I cannot judge the heart of the person." As you are speaking to your child, avoid tearing down the person, but rather calmly focus on the actions. Be ready to back this up scripturally. There are plenty of stories in the Bible on which a parent can draw to make a point. Continuously point your child's heart to the heart of God and his plans for that child's life.

Being a teen is so much about being accepted. Your child will be drawn to whatever or whomever they feel will accept them or help them to become acceptable. When teens look at a star they are looking at the outside, namely the money and the success. Help them to see there is something deeper. Something more.

BUT WHEN THE MIGHTY FALL?

We've encouraged you to remember the human frailty of idols and heartthrobs when you are talking to your teens and to point them toward Christian role models. But what happens when *Christians* fail?

We know it happens. I can think of a number of pastors, Christian athletes, Christian music artists, and Christian actors who have left their fans stunned and wounded. What's worse, their actions have resulted in young people doubting their own faith.

How is a parent to handle this? Again, with honesty. Now would be a good time to pull out the Word of God and talk about some biblical characters who—though they loved God—fell from grace on occasion. Or a lot!

Don't worry about where to begin. The Bible is full of men and women who wanted desperately to get it right—only to get it all wrong. But their stories are stories of God's grace, his mercy, and his redemption. You can always start with David. He's a favorite "fall guy" when it comes to this topic; God bless him!

> Teach your child to build his life on Jesus the Rock, rather than [people who are] "sinking sand," who are really just [flawed] like us.[11]
>
> —James Sang Li, movie stunt man, youth leader, parent

Be careful, though. You'll want to stress that just because God is faithful in his grace and mercy, this is not a ticket to sin. Teenagers often look for loopholes when it comes to their fleshly desires. Don't make this one of them. As you tell the stories of David and others, continue with the results of their sin. Then guide your teen in a discussion of how the current fallen idol is paying dearly.

I am reminded of a young Christian music artist who, a few years ago, was part of a new band that took the airwaves and tour circuits by storm. It seemed every time I turned on my radio, one of their songs was playing. Then, out of the blue, the sky caved in. Charges of sexual misconduct were placed on the lead singer. At first, many refused to believe it. But a tearful confession was made, and restitution was paid.

Sadly, however, the band broke up and was never heard from again. What appeared to be a fast ride to success quickly faded into another sad story in a long line of sad stories. Sadder still, hard as I try, I can remember neither the name of the band nor the name of the young man.

JESSICA'S BLOG

The commercial begins with P. Diddy, one of America's most powerful music moguls, dressed in a tux, standing next to a chauffeured luxury car broken down vehicle on the side of a long stretch of country highway. Heading down the road toward him is the only help in sight: a large Pepsi box truck. Desperate for a lift, he explains to the driver that he was on his way to an awards show when his vehicle broke down.

Next scene, Diddy arrives on the red carpet and climbs out the passenger side of said truck. Cameras start flashing. Everyone is oblivious to the fact that he has just hitchhiked to the awards show. As the commercial continues, we realize the full effect of his grand entrance. From coupes to pickups, every car on the road is now decorated just like the Pepsi box truck Diddy arrived in. Obviously mistaken as his latest vehicle, a car covered in a huge Pepsi logo is apparently the next big trend.

While a little extreme, what makes this commercial humorous is not that it's so ridiculous but because it's so true. Each of us, whether we realize it or not, draws some of our style or taste from popular culture—our celebrities, our icons. Who each of us chooses to be influenced by may vary based on whom we allow to entertain us. But in reality, popular culture is driven, created, and molded by icons and those who make them. As popular culture evolves, so do we.

So where do we find the line between living the American dream (and all that it has to offer) and living the life of the straight and narrow we were called to walk? Better yet, how will we help kids find it? How can we help them find that place where they can live for God with pride while maneuvering through all that is placed in their path?

To fully understand icons and their role in this whole thing, it would be good to start by looking at what makes them attractive. It is the job of celebrities and the people who help create them to know what will attract your kids. They know what will make the connection and make a teen feel a part of something. They know what works.

On top of that, celebrity status looks like the epitome of independence, which every teenager craves. A celebrity can appear to have everything the teen thinks he needs. For example, most teenaged boys desire three main things these days: money, power, and respect. What male icon doesn't emulate all three of these? The problem appears not because kids desire the success the stars have, but because they falsely believe that to achieve and acquire these things they should mimic the stars' behaviors. They fail to realize the self-destructive behavior of many stars is what makes them fall, not what makes them rise. Instead they feel the need to immerse themselves completely into the culture and lifestyle they admire to come closer to their ideal selves.

Role models are everywhere. There are role models for people of all ages. They're not necessarily positive role models, but they are role models nonetheless. There are even some who can promote both positive and negative lifestyles at the same time. How confusing is that?

The first thing I suggest is that you find out who is acting as your teen's role model. This may not be just a person. It could be an idea, a fad, a style, or a culture. But what are those things that get your teen "amped" and attentive? What people influence their style, taste in music, ideas about the world? When faced with tough decisions, whose thoughts and examples help them choose the best course of action? Who or what do they look to when things go wrong? Once you start to answer these questions, you can start to find out what examples they are leaving for your child.

Finally, be sure to point out or even arrange for your child to spend time with someone who is an example of what your teen would like to become (one who even has had the financial success that your child desires) yet still manages to walk a holy walk. Help him or her see that God doesn't want us to be broke and unsatisfied. Or to be lonely and out of touch with those around them. God doesn't want us to be sad, never laughing. No, he introduces us to what joy and success really are!

JESSICA'S Q & A BLOG

Since the 1950s, when being a teen became the most popular thing to be, media has produced idols or heartthrobs to inspire this age group.

NOW YOU TELL ME: WHAT DO YOU THINK IT IS ABOUT CELEBRITIES THAT DRAWS YOUNG PEOPLE?

Stephanie (nineteen, Colorado): I think we are so drawn to idols and heartthrobs because they are really good singers/actors or they are really bad, but very good-looking.

Sondra (fifteen, Washington): Everyone wants someone to look up to. People need someone they can respect, aspire to be or look like. Although it would be wonderful if teens and tweens would aspire to the fashion stylings of Condoleezza Rice, this doesn't happen. It takes much more effort to go to the library biography section and check out a book on Harriet Tubman or Sally Ride than to lie in your bed with *Seventeen* magazine.

Music artists and movie stars have such high media visibility. Even through watching the news at night, you see the faces of recording artists with their new reality show, or on a morning show promoting a new album.

Another attraction of music artists is they represent power and respect. Artists are able to speak their minds. They can say whatever they want and get away with it. Many times they even get praised for it. They have a power about them to get what they want. Teens and preteens need confirmation of how they are doing in life. *Am I cool enough? Am I wearing the right things? Do I look okay?* Musical artists are the ones who set the bar of where cool is. If you could just get to the level of many of them, you can then be accepted just as they are.

In today's society, producers and managers sell the person just as much as they sell the music. You rarely know every lyric and song on a CD when you buy it. You go to buy a CD with the image of the recording star in mind. When the person has a clean image, you buy the CD and then learn the way they express themselves is different from the image they show. But now that you have the CD you're not likely to throw it out.

Jessica (sixteen, Virginia): I think teenagers are drawn to music artists because of the life they portray. No problems, more money than anything, you can have whatever you want, it makes you want to do what that artist is doing, to become or to be as successful as that certain artist is. I am drawn to an artist by how I am affected by their songs. If a song brings out certain emotions in me or makes me think—that's what makes me think, *Well, maybe I should go get this artist's album to see what else he or she has to say.*

Lyrics are what catches a person off the back, not what the artist looks like or if they can dance, but what is being said in the song. Sex sells. Anything merely related to sex is caught in by DJs and talk show hosts as what's hot. An artist knows what's going to get them hot, and knows they are going to sell it. That just happens to be sex.

Sandy Austin (high school counselor, president Colorado School Counselor Association, and parent): I think it's because of the larger than life images these careers have—a fantasy teens can live out in their minds. Teens think life would be so much easier playing music or playing sports for the rest of their lives instead of another boring career. Since music or sports are typically fun things for kids, they have a positive view of those people. Hollywood and the media play a big role in that, too.

As far as the wholesome images that don't coincide with the sexual lyrics of the songs, I believe they can get away with it because the parents see the CD jackets and think the music must be okay. Few adults listen to the lyrics, watch MTV, or really know what is going on with their kids' music. The music industry's focus is on what sells. I remember when Madonna first came out with her blatantly sexual songs and even her sex book, she said she wanted to shock everyone—knowing people would buy the products just to see what was in them since they got such shocking reviews.

Last year at school I heard a girl singing along with a song on her iPod as she was waiting for another counselor. I couldn't believe what I heard, and I asked her if she realized the words she just belted out were about a violent sexual act. She said, "Not really, I just like the beat." I talked to her for a bit about it, but I don't think I changed her mind about listening to it.

Suzanne Eller (author, *Real Issues, Real Teens—What Every Parent Needs to Know*[12] and parent): If you listen to the music of any generation, you'll find within the lyrics the poetry of a generation. Teens are drawn to them because they're speaking something they are feeling.

It's also part of finding their own identity. I believe that teens want to know who they are. They want to explore their roles in the world—in their family, in their faith, in society, with friends, and with the opposite sex. Music is a powerful and influential resource—whether that is negative or positive—in that search.

James Li (actor/stunt man, youth leader, and parent): I think there are many reasons why young people are so drawn to celebrities but I will give just three. First, because God has given us all a built-in sense and desire for worship. It is not always directed toward him, but it is this worship that is designed to be toward him ("Love the Lord your God with all your heart, mind, soul").

Second, we all have a great need to belong, and it is this belief that many times defines how we act. Whether that is to dress like teen pop culture stars, purchase certain cars or gadgets, or hang around with certain kinds of people, it comes back to the need for acceptance.

Third, young people know how to have fun and desire to be part of what is happening and what is exciting. They have humanitarian issues as well as spiritual questions on their minds and are looking for guides to direct them. Celebrities have the platforms to convey both excitement and causes in their tours and media exposure, which can attract young people.

CHAPTER 3

Sex, Lies, and Fashion

Or, A Bread Crumb & Fish

In the March 30, 2005, showing of Oprah, guest Jada Pinkett Smith tells a story of the day her four-year-old Willow wanted to wear a midriff top so she'd be "sexy." Jada responded with, "Does Mommy have to dress like that to be sexy for Daddy?" Willow replied, "No." "Then," Jada said, "you don't either."

I couldn't help myself! I had to laugh. Written across the chest of the new T-shirt were these words: Abreadcrumb & Fish. Underneath the slogan read: Jesus Christ + Miracle Worker.

So what made this girl giggle? The parody of the catchphrase was on Abercrombie & Fitch, America's number one clothier of young people. The Christian T-shirt people had taken a blight against our youth and turned it into a positive witness.

WHO ARE ABERCROMBIE & FITCH?

To prepare to write this section, I typed "Abercrombie & Fitch" into a search engine of the Internet. As the numerous sites concerning the store came up, I noticed that on the left side of the screen, which allows one to "narrow their search," the following words were listed:

- Catalog
- Sex
- ANF
- Brand, Clothing
- Boycott
- Lawsuit

Um … what was that second word again? *Sex?* What does sex have to do with clothing? Abercrombie & Fitch have taken "sex sells" to a whole new level. While researching our book *Sex, Lies, and the Media,* I was reminded that sex is used to sell everything from "bubblegum to toothpaste," as one young lady so aptly put it. Not that I truly had to be reminded. But, when my research took me to A&F and to their magalog (a magazine/catalog), which I easily purchased for $7.00 in a local mall, I learned that—for some odd reason—sex *and nudity* sell clothing.

Was it always this way with the company? No. A&F began over a hundred years ago as a small waterfront shop and factory in New York City. Then known as David T. Abercrombie Co., it was a supplier of rugged outdoor gear. Just under a century later, it was bought by The Limited, Inc., and four years after that was repositioned as a more fashion-oriented business.

History lesson over. Today there are hundreds of Abercrombie & Fitch stores in the United States. The merchandise focus is on collegiate men and women with a new target audience for children and teenagers in stores like Abercrombie Kids and Hollister Co., which was introduced in 2000.

And of course, there is *the magalog.*

> Forty-five specific portrayals of sexual imagery in the first 120 pages … this is how the new Abercrombie & Fitch quarterly titled "The Christmas Field Guide" begins its new quarterly magazine that is targeted to your ten- to thirteen-year-olds. The forty-five images include overt portrayals of group sex, lots of teen and young adult nudity, men kissing, and teens/young adults frolicking in a river engaging in sexual activity in multiple group settings. Did I mention that the actual clothing doesn't begin being advertised until page 120?[1]
>
> —Kevin McCullough, writer, WorldNetDaily.com

RECENTLY ...

In the past few years, Abercrombie & Fitch has managed to raise more than a few eyebrows, infuriate a boatload of parents, and ignite concern among Christian coalitions. In 2003, A&F released their now-infamous *Back to School* magalog. Its matte-finish cover displayed three reportedly college-age naked teens—two males and one female—climbing into a convertible car. All necessary "parts" were carefully hidden by other not so necessary parts.

Within the pages of the magalog are nearly 150 pages of sexual escapades; many between these three, but also including others and including scenes of orgies. Somewhere between pages 140 and 150, A&F's *Back to School* issue becomes (finally) about fashion. But later—in the back—articles concerning sex and campus life prevail. All this for $7.00.

Parental advocacy groups revolted, and when the Christmas issue was released a few months later, they became hysterical. Along with sexually explicit images, the company's "Christmas Field Guide" informed young people in no uncertain terms that "there are no sexual boundaries and no consequences to any sexual behavior," according to the National Coalition for the Protection of Children and Families.[2]

But when A&F developed a line of thong panties for ten-year-old girls with messages like "Eye Candy" written on them and designed to be worn outside the tops of their jeans, the company had crossed the line, come back, and crossed it again. The outcry from parents could be heard straight to Ohio, where A&F's headquarters is located.

The problem here is that the number-one clothier of young people is advocating group sex, oral sex, heterosexual and homosexual sex ... well, you get the gist of what I'm trying to say. The focus quickly became more about taking clothes *off* rather than putting them on. And our young people—even our Christian young people—were buying into the lie that being young and free is about all these things. How often I've walked into churches across the country, whether in my own church or as a guest speaker, only to see the A&F logo stitched or pressed into the fabrics of the clothes worn by those in attendance.

And I think: *How can you support this?* Just as quickly, I answer: *Because, chances are you don't know everything I know.*

Then, just as quickly, I wonder how anyone *can't* know. The walls of A&F are plastered with larger than life nude photos of young people. The brand itself carries a line of T-shirts called "Sex Appeal," imprinted with slogans like *Buck Fuddy*[3] and *Your Mom Serves Great Flap Jacks.*

> Sex is what corporate America uses to sell to teens. If you watch enough TV, you'll start to think that the whole world is having wild threesomes, and you'll feel pretty bad about your own sex life.[4]
>
> —Ned Vizzini, author of *Teen Angst?*

Abercrombie & Fitch's money-making executives have cashed in on a fact few of us realize: Teens and young adults wear clothes for three reasons: *utility*, *status*, and *sex*. In other words, to protect themselves from weather elements, to establish a sense of style and presence, and to say, "Look at me. I'm sexy."

I WANNA LOOK LIKE ...

It will come as no surprise to you as a parent when I say that sexual messages in teen dress are greatly influenced by media personalities and by media advertising. Personalities in both music and the movies direct their appeal to their youthful audience. They work hard to stay young looking. No one in their right mind says, "I want to appeal to the masses by looking old and unattractive." The problem is, we've somehow connected *appeal* only with *sex*.

One of the reasons we began this book with a talk about icons is their influence in so many areas of your teen's life, including dress and style. Teens and tweens borrow the clothing styles of those actors and singers they want to imitate. This is a trend that didn't begin yesterday. It dates back to the beginning of modern media. Veronica Lake (the Peak-a-Boo girl, so-called for the way her hair dipped across her forehead and over one eye) was copied for her sexy hairstyle. Marilyn Monroe's stiletto heels were the sexy style of her day. Though he didn't live long, James Dean made a huge impression on young men with a "bad boy" image. Twiggy's nearly emaciated physique was considered hot in the 1960s, as was Marlo Thomas's "That Girl" look.

But today's youth are driven to distraction by the likes of Britney and Jessica, Christina and Beyoncé. Sexuality and fashion is mainly a girl thing, which in turn affects boys greatly. Especially young men who are working to stay pure before God. As one young man said to me, "It's not impossible, but girls sure don't make it easy for us."

AN INTERESTING ARTICLE

I came across an interesting article written by Dannah Gresh, author of *And the Bride Wore White* and *Secret Keeper: The Delicate Power of Modesty*,[5] which tells of a time when her husband, Bob, author of *Who Moved the Goalpost*,[6] quizzed a group of Christian teen boys. "What's the number one thing that causes you to feel sexually tempted?" he asked them.

According to the article "The Fashion Battle: Is It Worth Fighting?"[7] the boys wasted no time giving him an answer. By far … the worst thing … (are you ready for this?) "… the way girls dress in church." Not the media or the Internet. Girls in church.

One of the young men added, "It's like church is *supposed* to be a place where you don't have to face temptation and you walk in and … bam! There it is."

What makes Christian young women want to dress in ways that do little to promote their femininity and the core of their essence and way too much to promote themselves as *only* being a toy?

That's an easy question to answer: advertising.

The average North American girl will watch 5,000 hours of television, including 80,000 ads before she starts kindergarten.[8] The message media hands out to these girls is so mixed up, it's no wonder they have a difficult time as teens learning to express themselves as individuals. They end up working feverishly to take on the look and the sensuality of the models within the glossy ads. Sadly, the models employed for such ads are getting younger and younger ... and their images sexier and sexier.

> You have heard that it was said, "Do not commit adultery." But I tell you that anyone who looks at a woman lustfully has already committed adultery with her in his heart.
>
> —Matthew 5:27–28

Remember, if sex sells, and the clothiers want to make the sale, then using sexuality will become the means to the end.

IT'S NOT JUST A&F

My research led me to another clothier, one for girls only.

Candies, known for hot fashions, such as shoes, apparel, and accessories, has launched a teen pregnancy awareness campaign, complete with little T-shirts that read, *Be Sexy; It doesn't mean you have to have sex.*

At the Candies Web site, young girls can view various stars (there are those icons again) modeling the shirts. The problem is (1) some of these stars promote sexuality by virtue of their very work and (2) their poses are alluring and inviting.

Another problem is that the icon leading teen boys and girls to this section of the Web site is a close-up of a large-breasted woman wearing the T-shirt. Actually, all you see are the *breasts*.

While I'm sure Candies' intent is honorable, the fact is, teaching teens about abstinence and/or safe sex and teaching them about sexual integrity are two different things. Part of sexual integrity for girls is wearing nothing that would knowingly cause a young man's eyes to sin. For if his eyes sin, then his mind. And if his mind, then his heart.

SO WHAT'S THE DEAL WITH SEX BRACELETS?

I was standing in line at a Barnie's Coffee and Tea kiosk, scanning the list of liquid delicacies with my eyes and eavesdropping with my ears on the conversation between a mother and daughter who stood in front of me. (I'm a mother. I can multitask.)

From what I could ascertain, the mother had just purchased a set of "jelly bracelets" for her daughter. As the young girl fingered the circles of various colors, she was informing the mother, "We're not allowed to wear these at school."

"Well, that's just silly," the mother said. "Why in the world not?"

The child shrugged her shoulders and said, "I dunno. We just can't."

It was at this point that I looked down to the girl who, instinctively, looked up at me. I winked, gave a sideward grin, and mouthed, "You know."

She smiled back at me, then rolled her eyes.

She and I knew what the mother did not. And maybe as a parent you don't either. After you read this, you won't be able to say that.

SEX BRACELET, YOU SAY?

Made popular in the '80s by Madonna, jelly bracelets are inexpensive and colorful soft-plastic bangles that have made a comeback.

And they're causing quite a stir. According to what could just be folk-lore, based on their color, they represent willingness to perform specific sexual acts. Different regions or groups of people say the colors mean different things, but they all seem to agree that black means sexual intercourse.

Or, as it turns out, they could just be bracelets.

There's been such controversy around this issue, and—according to news releases across America—adults have been as confused as students. While some teens say the bracelets are only fashion statements, others say they are about sex and sex parties (the game most popularly referred to is called "Snap"). Some school and church youth officials won't allow them to be worn, others don't see a problem.

Bottom line, as far as I can tell, is that it's whatever your teen wants it to be. That's where you have to step in and talk to your child or to your child's school. If you have any doubts, err on the side of safety.

MODESTY AND SEXUAL INTEGRITY

Teaching your children about modesty and sexual integrity includes helping your daughter make wise choices in dress and helping your son find ways to avoid the pitfalls as best he can.

FOR YOUR DAUGHTERS:

If you are the parent of a high school daughter, pay attention to what is in her closet. This is not a time for criticism but rather a time for bonding. One thing most mothers and daughter agree on is the need for clothing.

If you are not a shopper by nature and your daughter is, come out of your comfort zone. Take the time to look through fashion magazines and to talk openly about why certain styles will or will not work with your daughter, whether due to her body type or for modesty's sake. Allow her to be real with *you*, too. Even at the young age of seven, my granddaughter—when we're shopping together—is quick to say things like, "That's not your color," should I pull something off the rack that she finds unappealing for me.

Take trips to the mall or to boutiques together. Make it more than a chore. Enjoy a movie or a stop at a candle shop or even a stop at a café for a Coke. Find something your daughter enjoys and incorporate it.

If your daughter is not a shopper and you are, try shopping online or by catalog. Again, make it memorable and bonding, rather than a fate worse than death.

> Charm is deceptive, and beauty is fleeting; but a woman who fears the Lord is to be praised.
> —Proverbs 31:30

As difficult as it can be these days to find fashionable clothes that don't reveal "all the possibilities," it can be done. Remember, however, that you as the parent have the final say. You may not be able to control what they put on once they are out of eyeshot, but you can set your boundaries. In the end, they will respect that.

There's another point that demands to be made. Your role as a parent—or at least one of them—is to teach your daughter that beauty does not come from fashion or makeup or even a great hairstyle. These enhance beauty, but they do not create it. Beauty comes from deep within..

That beauty can best be defined as *elegance.* If you have examples of this within your community, church, or family, point them out. Look especially to an older woman with whom your daughter might have rapport, one she finds beautiful in spite of the marks of time. Ask the woman to show your daughter photos of herself in her younger days. This will show—rather than tell—your daughter that outward, youthful beauty truly is fleeting, but inward loveliness will last a lifetime.

Next, the subject of fashion, modesty, and sexuality is an opportune time for you to talk to your daughter about her worth as an individual ... not as a boy toy. While they may be the most popular on Friday and Saturday nights, by Sunday morning, the "easy girls" are used goods. And while—when the need arises—the teen boy may call her for a quick date (and I think you get my meaning here), he won't consider her for anything more than a physical release. Impress upon your daughter her worth, in the eyes of you, in the eyes of others, in her own eyes, and in the eyes of God.

Finally, remember that the way a young girl dresses or desires to dress may be an outward sign of inward insecurities. If your daughter is struggling with right and wrong choices or you fear she may have been sexually compromised in some way, seek counsel.

FOR YOUR SONS:

How possible is it to maintain sexual integrity when you are swimming in a pool full of half-dressed sharks? I'm sure, for our sons, it feels this way sometimes. So much of the answer to this question depends on the state of mind and level of spiritual maturity of your son. I know grown men who couldn't handle the temptations that come with seeing the sexual immodesty of young or adult women.

While we have a list of resources at the end of this book designed to help with this topic and others, one way you may want to approach your son is with something he can understand, especially if he is sports minded. You can tell him that a coach of any sport worth his paycheck would never send his team out on the field or into a stadium without a game *plan*. Encourage your son to have a "God-help-me-stay-pure" plan drawn up and ready for the game.

One young man told me he has a song he sings to himself every time he is tempted. "I figure that the temptation comes from the devil anyway, so my plan is to beat him at his own game," he told me. "When some girl comes walking by with a short skirt or with her breast—even a little of it—exposed, I start singing this song in my head. It's an old one we've always sung at church, but it works. "Praise God from whom all blessings flow."[9] He laughed as he sang off key. "It works. Every time, it works."

Sounds good to me!

JESSICA'S BLOG

It is true that some of the provocative fashions of today are compromising for young ladies and a temptation to young men. More than that, they are reflections of the lifestyles of our youth. We don't act the way we act because of the clothes we wear, in more cases than not we wear what we wear because of the lives we live. The rain doesn't start because someone put on a raincoat; we put our raincoats on because it starts raining!

So the sense of fashion that your teenager has will be more of a reflection of her lifestyle—more a symptom than a root cause. So rather than just say, "No way are you wearing that outfit out of this house," or even, "Aren't you going to do something with yourself before you leave?" see her clothes as a form of expression of not only how she feels, but also what type of lifestyle she is trying to lead or emulate.

Not to say that you should allow them to wear anything they want because it is just a reflection or an expression. While they are under your protection, they are just that: under your protection. It is up to you to protect them by any means necessary, even if that means making them angry or "hate you." But it shouldn't stop there. Because if the clothes you and your teen disagree on are an indication of a more serious danger, then regulating what clothes she wears out of your house is just the beginning and a way to help keep things from getting any worse. You still have their core beliefs, values, goals, and opinions to consider.

Chances are when you try to discuss issues about their clothing (or lack of) you both will feel you aren't on the same page. That's because you're not, and you're not going to be. While you will stress the morality and maturity issues, they will probably look at you like you're crazy because "For crying out loud, it's just a shirt!"

True, it's not that there's something evil about the clothes, but more the situations these kinds of styles put young people in. It may be something more mature adults could handle or choose for themselves, but a teenager doesn't know enough to handle a decision like that. They don't even know enough to know they don't know enough.

For instance, a teen girl doesn't know how to receive the feedback she would get from wearing a miniskirt. (And she will get feedback.) Will she learn to think that if she gets more compliments in the miniskirt than the church dress, then the miniskirt must be the way to go? Will she realize what the skirt will make her valued for and all that entails? Will she be able to read between the lines of the hoots and hollers and see down to the end of that road in the way you can? Will she know what to do when all the compliments have found her alone in a room with a hormone-driven boy or man? I would be willing to bet the answer is no.

Now maybe there is a time and a place for a grown woman to appropriately wear, let's say for instance, the "little black dress." But is there ever one for an adolescent girl? I'd be hard pressed to think of one. Teenaged Jessica would've disagreed. Adult Jessica sees things differently.

But hey, that's part of raising a teenager.

There must be a way to protect your children from these dangers while still making them feel like you're giving them the space they need to express their style, make mistakes, learn and grow from them. There must be a way to counteract this issue beyond force and forbidding. This begins with your ability to help them unmask the lies they are being told about their beauty. It also begins with teaching young men to seek out attractive young women who value themselves enough to leave something to the imagination.

A time will come in a young girl's life when she begins to care how people view her physically. And these days that time is coming younger and younger. Too young, if you ask me; there are eight-year-olds on diets these days! Hopefully they have already had self-confidence instilled in them at home and will not feel the need to get it elsewhere. But no matter how much you have validated your children at home, not many teenage girls would resent being complimented for their shape or some other attractive feature. This is exactly why girls like to dress provocatively.

Teen boys are practically infested with scantily dressed young ladies. They're everywhere. And these days, many teen girls look as grown and developed as women twice their age. No wonder male middle and high school teachers are suddenly finding their job such a challenge! So if you're this teen boy struggling with your own weaknesses (in reality most are succumbing, not struggling) and are constantly surrounded by all this "eye candy" (even at church!), how much more difficult would it be for you to spot an attractive but conservatively dressed young lady across the room?

Teen girls experience it every day. It is difficult to walk with your girlfriend down the halls of school and listen to all the praise she receives because of how she looks, while you feel as though you must be completely invisible. Or find yourself standing alone all the time because guys are constantly trying to "holla" your friend when the two of you are hanging out. The next day when you get dressed, you are remembering that feeling. And that feeling is going to influence your choice of clothing.

It is now a cycle. Girls are going to dress sexy to get the attention of boys, and boys are going to have a hard time diverting their attention from them as long as they keep walking around like this. Unless some wisdom and understanding are gradually impressed in our youth, lust will soon take over their lives.

So we're back to fighting the problem. A cycle has to be attacked from all sides. As long as our young men continue to come up viewing women as sexual objects rather than as jewels to be treasured, girls (and women) will continue to debase themselves for attention. Because women are born attention-junkies. It takes maturity to learn to be your own source of attention and praise. Maybe you know all this already, but your kids don't. Even if they have started to understand, they still need continued support and encouragement in this area.

Women, we need to be examples not only to young men of what a woman of God can become, but also to young women. Ask them: Who are you and what are you striving to become? What sets you apart? What gifts are you going to be able to give your future husband by being the woman God has called you to be? When those same boys start looking for a meaningful relationship, they will only be interested in someone they can respect.

When this starts to make sense to them, ask them to describe themselves and how they think other people would describe them. It is the ability to examine oneself that will allow them to keep balanced during progressively changing years.

Men, we need you as much as (if not more than) women in this battle. This is because of the radically influential role you could play in not only a boy's but also a girl's understanding and experience with physical beauty. Boys begin to decide what is the purpose of a female in their life at a young age. Their views are nurtured by the male (and female) role models in their lives and by the media when role models aren't present. If you are a role model to young men, be a mentor of godly influence and encouragement.

A good friend of mine is the father of a beautiful ten-year-old daughter. Although they no longer share the same residence, he is a huge part of her everyday life. They live minutes away from each other, and he often will go over after work and just sit with her while she does her homework. (And this is a man who works a seventy-hour work week.) One of her friends is a little girl whose father, sadly, is not in the picture. She is aware of this fact and often wonders to my friend why her daddy can't be more like him. Recently the three of them were spending playtime together when this same little girl asked him to be her "pretend daddy." He looked down at the shirt she was wearing: a simple white T-shirt with the silhouette of the Playboy bunny. He told her if she wanted him to act like her daddy then get up and change her shirt. Of course at ten years old she couldn't fully understand why. Even after he explained briefly that the shirt would cause boys to look at her as something to use and take advantage of, she still didn't have a complete understanding of the issue. But what a beautiful start! She was just like any other young girl, starving for male attention. Thank God she was finally fed the kind she deserves.

When it comes to our young girls, lessons on dressing properly are much easier to swallow coming from a guy. A woman tells us not to dress sexy and women's deep-seated competitive nature will form a natural wall. We don't like to take advice from the "enemy," especially when that enemy is Mom. Besides, what could she know about this kind of stuff? Coming from a man (like a father, uncle, or father figure) in an honest, up-front fashion that tells the truth about the way boys are, the message will sink in. Your influence can be a beautiful thing. Positive male role models are too few and far between.

Men, please (I beg you), take the time out of your busy schedules to mold the values and understanding of a young person, boy or girl. A little at a time all along the way will produce a well-adjusted young adult with a great head on his or her shoulders.

Last but not least, don't forget to tell your kids every day how beautiful they are, stressing their authentic beauty. Tell what makes them remarkable children of God. Point out specific qualities they can control. Reinforce good behavior, opinions, and choices they make in regard to their own self-respect and respecting their relationships with the opposite sex. If you remember to do all these things in little ways over and over again, you will raise a well-balanced, levelheaded young adult. Put them all together, and we have changed a generation!

Back to Abreadcrumb & Fish

Remember the beginning of this chapter when we talked about the Christian T-shirt with *Abreadcrumb & Fish* written on it? Well, I want to go back to that.

In the story of Jesus and the miracle of the five thousand we read of the day when Jesus had been preaching to the multitudes. They got hungry, but when Jesus sent the disciples out to determine how much food was among the throng, they came back with a gloomy report. There were only five loaves of bread and two fish, a common lunch in their day. Jesus blessed the food, broke it, and had the disciples pass it around. When all were filled, there were twelve full baskets left over (John 6:1–13).

Jesus takes the simplest things and makes them spectacular.

The next time your children bemoan their lack of fashion sense or complain because they aren't able to dress like everyone else in the crowd, remind them of this story. They are taking on the clothing of righteousness. What may seem ordinary and common to them, when placed in the hands of Jesus, is spectacular.

Jessica's Q & A Blog

Now you tell me: How difficult is it for guys today to maintain their sexual purity of sight and mind (not to mention just plain ol' purity!) with girls' fashions being as they are?

Justin (eighteen, Kentucky): Well there are plenty of popular name brands that sell "non-suggestive clothing," but for the most part the suggestive look is what's popular now. Girls are constantly dressing more risky these days and for one reason, to get noticed. These girls aren't dressing sexy because that's all they can buy nowadays, but because that's what guys are looking for. When a girl dresses risky, what she is saying is "Hey, I bet you like this, approach me." It's like leaving the cookie jar open on the floor with a little kid around. They are using it as a way to get the interest of a male.

Most males are going to notice, and if the girl is attractive, then they will appreciate it. Some guys will approach these girls and some won't. Most girls who take it too far will attract an aggressive male. Now the guys don't have a reasonable argument either. If a guy doesn't want to look at a female in an erotic way, he doesn't have to. Most guys like when a girl dresses that way, and they will look. To them it's innocent porn. They think, "If they are going put it out there, then I am going to look."

I wouldn't say it's hard to stay pure, but I also wouldn't say it's easy. It isn't as hard to stay pure in a *physical* way, but *mentally* I would beg to differ. When you see a plate and a fork, you're going to think about food, and when you see an attractive young female, you're more than likely going to think about sex. Keep in mind you don't have to look, even though most teen males are looking for girls. When I see a pretty girl, my mind will involuntarily register that she is attractive, but after that it's up to me.

Dale (fifteen, Tennessee): It is always difficult for a guy to maintain purity even if girls are dressed modestly, but it does add to the *level* of difficulty when you are exposed to *immoralness*, if I can use that as a word.

Christine (sixteen, Virginia): Modesty is something we were discussing a few weeks ago when we went to Centrifuge during our church devotion. We got into a heated argument over what modesty is. We were split, and I said that I dress modestly because I want to, but that modesty is determined by a person's personal beliefs. I believe wearing clothes that show anything that is suggestive, such as a lot of cleavage where you can see down the shirt or really short shorts that only stop where the legs end, is a little too much.

My biggest thing is girls wearing these clothes on purpose instead of out of necessity. I don't get how anyone says it's hard to find comfortable, fashionable, modest clothes when it's sitting on the shelves, being looked over just because it's not the modern view of what is fashionable. My friend from my church, Tony, said that he doesn't like his girlfriend wearing those things for the sake of wearing them because it makes it seem that she could slip away from him that much easier and is inviting other guys to look at her.

The guys in my church all say that if a girl with skimpy clothes came in the room, they would get to know the girl to find out why the girl was insecure enough to feel like she has to dress this way. If clothes stores that sell these skimpy clothes pulled out some hemlines and made more reasonable clothes available EVERYWHERE, then we wouldn't have any of the problems we're having with girls and skimpy clothes.

Also, I think that if actresses didn't wear the barely-there clothes to fashionable events, such as the MTV Movie Awards or the Oscars, then it would set a better example. Celebrities wear these clothes to get attention.

Brian (seventeen, Southern California): Actually, it is hard to maintain purity. The females with the jeans that barely go above anything and the shirts that barely cover anything. But I see the answer as easy as this: If you really want to have your relationship with God "work," then you have to just put your mind to it. If you want your relationship to run smooth with Jesus, you just have to bite the bullet. Of course, you are gonna slip up because no one is perfect, and you're gonna have some trials, but you just have to repent and start from there.

NOW YOU TELL ME: IS IT POSSIBLE FOR GIRLS TO DRESS MODESTLY AND FASHIONABLY AT THE SAME TIME?

Jill Swanson (author of *Simply Beautiful Inside and Out*, parent): YES! I think the answer comes first of all in the fit. Often a teen does one of two things, chooses clothing that is either too big or too tight. The large clothing isn't much of an issue when it comes to modesty;

however, it does tend to make the wearer appear sloppy, sending out an I-don't-care message.

"Tight" would include anything that reveals telltale signs of undergarments or pieces that "smile" at you because they are strained (a T-shirt that is too tight and has horizontal waves across the bust and jeans or pants that pull to a ripple below the waistband are indicators that there is stress in the fabric where it shouldn't be).

The answer comes in finding pieces that gently skim the body and move with you without restricting or revealing. Clothes that subtly silhouette the figure without showcasing the anatomy can be attractive without being overtly sexy. A small percentage (2–5 percent) of spandex can work well in a sweater to help it maintain its shape and not cling too tightly.

A better quality fabric is also a good idea. Most clothes manufactured for adolescents are cheap, and while the cotton T-shirt may fit perfectly when you put it on in the store, one washing can shrink a size ten to a two. Manufacturers do this to keep costs low and appeal to the conspicuous consumption of the young consumer. One option is to consider shopping for your basics (white shirt, black camisole, tan pants) in the ladies department or go with better brands, such as Lands End or Ralph Lauren (while expensive at first, the cost per wearing is more economical in the long run).

Clothing that floats with the body is also a beautiful way to show femininity. The popular full skirts and chiffon overlays in dresses and blouses are a good example of this.

Another option to looking great without sacrificing modesty is wearing colors that flatter your features. Finding a shirt or sweater that matches your lip and cheek color, such as pink, peach, or rose, can be attracting to the opposite sex. The same is true of your eye color. Choosing a blue dress to match the blue of your iris will have him mesmerized by your eyes and hanging on your every word (after all, having eye contact enhances your communication skills!).

If it's attention the girl wants, she can do it modestly with color. A solid bright color from head to toe can look stunning and will upstage any tight or revealing piece her peers may be displaying that season.

Most men will tell you it is sexier to subtly cover up than to blatantly exhibit your bumps and curves.

Allison Bottke (former model, author of *A Stitch in Time—Confessions of a Plastic Surgery Junkie*[10] and parent): In the world of fashion, the key words are *trendy*, *edgy*, and *current*. Just look at issues of fashion magazines over the past decade to see how fickle the "look of the moment" really is. Staying on top of what's "in" and what's "out" is a fun pastime, a fun hobby. But it should never be the basis on which we judge others or ourselves. Inner beauty is timeless. Inner beauty will leave its mark long after the fashion of the moment has moved on. If a young woman truly wants to leave a room and still be remembered, it's not going to be her external looks that folks will long recall—it's going to be what she said, what she didn't say, and how kind and loving she was. A truly beautiful woman with a heart of stone is quickly forgotten, whereas a woman with a heart that cares is long remembered, whether her shoes are from Prada or Payless, her dress from Valentino or JC Penney, or her make-up from Sephora or Maybelline.

Terri Brown (Christian high school teacher, parent): A girl who understands the idea of sexual purity won't wear jeans that barely cover her front because she knows exposing too much skin takes away from a guy's sexual purity. A teenaged boy today is bombarded with visual images that can diminish his sexual purity. But the responsibility is his to protect his mind. This may mean that he doesn't hang around a girl's locker after school or at lunch during the school day. Although he will definitely still see cleavage and belly button rings in everyday life, he can try to manipulate his environment to some degree.

But can I add that boys today must also go out of their way to avoid some overly aggressive girls? I can't say enough that parents must get involved if they are to truly help their teens. Not taking calls from girls, developing a dress code for girls that visit the house (if at all), and setting guidelines for a teen boy to know what is honorable behavior for a girl are not bad ideas.

When I was coming up through school, I thought some of the female leaders at my church were totally strict. But those standards are still with me today. It's just a different generation that needs to be taught.

CHAPTER 4

Sex, Lies, and Spring Break

Or, Has Anyone Ever Heard of Dionysus?

Just think, 20,000 kids out there.
Yeah, and 80 percent of them boys.

—Yvette Mimieux and Connie Francis
in the 1960s film *Where the Boys Are* (MGM)

I t's spring break. Do you know where your kids are?

Speaking of high school … do you remember taking a course called Greek Mythology? If so, are you able to bring to mind a chap named Dionysus?

According to the ancient folklore, Dionysus was the son of Zeus, the king of the gods. In part, the worship of Dionysus involved the ecstatic and was linked to the ingestion of the hallucinogenic fly agaric (poisonous mushroom), *Amanita muscaria*. He was called the god of wine, the god of drunkenness, and the god of ecstasy.

The legend states that each winter Dionysus died only to be reborn in the spring of the following year. So each year, the Greeks would celebrate this resurrection of sorts with dramas, competitions, orgies, and drinking until the participants were (to borrow from today's language) "wasted."

In a letter to his friend Cosima Wagner, Friedrich Nietzsche [a German philosopher who coined the phrase "God is dead" and who wrote the books *On the Genealogy of Morals* (1887) and *The Anti-Christ* (1888)] wrote, "This time however I come as the victorious Dionysus, who will turn the world into a holiday."[1]

In the Middle Ages, Christianity brought the revelry to something resembling a halt. Still, young people managed to party every spring, whether they had a sound reason or not.

In 1237, the church proposed taking the uncontrolled seasonal rite of passage and turning it into something decent and orderly. History has to hand it to them; they tried. Tried, but failed.

The word *rave* comes from ancient Greek texts describing the behavior of intoxicated dancers and followers of Dionysus.[2]

Our country's early settlers weren't in for the spring-break craze. I suppose they were too busy relocating. The contemporary American spring-break experience originated with the college crowd as far back as the early nineteenth century. In those days women were not a part of the collegiate picture, but the affluent male student would use the holiday for traveling to the coast or a nearby retreat for a little rest and relaxation from the stresses of campus life.

The twentieth century brought girls on campus and the automobile, so "road trip" now meant more than getting-away time spent with the boys. What could be better than a week away from professors, house parents, or even real parents, with members of the opposite sex?

During World War I, American soldiers serving in France were introduced to the ancient "get-naked" celebration, though the craze didn't catch on right away. From about 1930 to about 1960, America was dealing with some fairly difficult days, leaving behind that urge to party hardy. It's amazing what a Great Depression and a few wars can do to people.

Then a new era occurred in the 1960s. Society and morality were slackening, and movies of teens frolicking on our coastline beaches were produced. Spring break was back. And while it began as a collegiate activity, it quickly caught on with high school students who were ready, willing, and able to imitate their elder counterparts.

WHERE THE BOYS ARE

Some dialogue in the 1960 blockbuster teen movie *Where the Boys Are* is just too perfect not to pass along when writing about spring break. The scene opens with a motorcycle cop puttering up to Fort Lauderdale's city hall building where a cluster of officers have gathered at the front steps. The chief of police is addressing his men, saying,

> Gentlemen, the city of Fort Lauderdale is once again under fire from the north. We've survived it before, and I reckon we're gonna survive it again. To you newly installed officers who've never seen action in the war against higher education, I'd like to give you a little rundown on what to expect. Expect anything. Anything and everything, because that's what you're gonna get.... The students of America are gathering together to celebrate the rites of spring ... they have that right. They're our future voters, they're citizens of our country, and they are our responsibility. [He pauses, sighs deeply.] But how to handle them, that's a different matter.

So what are our children up to during spring break?

SPRING BREAK MENU

I spent an awful (and I do mean *awful*) lot of time watching all the spring-break specials television could offer during spring 2005. And I read a lot of magazine articles, newspaper reports, etc. That said, I've come to a pretty solid conclusion: Our kids have just gone nuts. (*Wait!* Didn't my parents' generation say pretty much the same thing about mine?) Allow me to share with you just a few of the escapades I've witnessed on television or read about.

- Dare Games, i.e., for money, pretty girls suck whipped cream off the toes of other pretty girls, they also lick whipped cream off the chests of boys they've not previously met, or off racecars, etc.
- Wet T-shirt Contests
- Underwear Contests
- Swimsuit Contests
- Hot Body Contests
- "Show Me Your Breasts" (FYI: According to one source, this element of spring break began in World War I when Doughboys were fighting in the trenches of France. To continue their annual fest, European soldiers dressed as women to entertain the war-weary boys. "Show Me Your Breasts" was a way to determine whether the dancer was male or female.[3])
- Co-ed Kiss Fests
- Spring Break Kiss-O-Rama (where two to four people kiss each other simultaneously)
- Drinking Contests
- General experimentation with drugs, sex, and sexuality

> Let me tell you about the little girl walking out with the T-shirt on. Everyone's quiet, right? But I knew something was going to erupt. She was like a volcano, building and building. It was like everybody knew. You could feel rumblings. You just didn't know when it was going to explode. Holy h*ll, was that a show! Holy h*ll![4]
>
> —Sean William Scott, talking about a girl who wore a long T-shirt in a spring-break contest (in which the actor was a celebrity observer), took it off, and revealed that she was naked underneath.[5]

ARE THEY MATURE ENOUGH TO UNDERSTAND THE DANGERS?

Though she was not on spring break at the time, Natalee Holloway's story has shaken parents and given a wake-up call to students across the world. Natalee, a graduating honors student from Birmingham, Alabama, disappeared on May 30, 2005, during a senior trip on the island of Aruba.

Americans—and the world—were glued to television sets, wondering what might have happened to the pretty blonde. The hearts of parents and grandparents broke at the sight of Natalee's family as they begged for information. Students wondered why an intelligent young woman would take such a chance to break away from the crowd and hook up with three island boys who—at the writing of this book—were believed to be the last to see her. Many could not understand how a bright and pretty girl from a loving family possibly could have made such a choice.

> The dangerous thing about spring break is that you get a strong sense of freedom from being away from your home environment. Partying out of town or around people with whom you don't normally associate gives you the feeling that you can do anything and it won't really count.
>
> —Jessica Everson

While teenagers, in particular high school seniors, feel they are grown-up and responsible, the fact is they are still highly unaware of the world's dangers. During excursions such as spring break and senior trips, teens will typically take on the "grown-up" activity of drinking. When they drink in excess, their defenses are cut nearly to nothing and their decision-making processes are weakened. Break down the ability to make logical choices, and you have the recipe for disaster.

According to an ABC TV news broadcast (during their annual spring-break exposé), by midafternoon teenagers enjoying the holiday were "fall-down drunk and incoherent."[6] There is a higher treatment rate of alcohol poisoning and alcohol-related injuries at hospitals and clinics during spring break.

According to a University of Wisconsin study, few students who had sex during spring break used condoms, even if a condom was available.[7] Anonymous sex, which can lead to unwanted pregnancy and life-altering STDs, is common during spring break. According to the same University of Wisconsin study, among women, those with higher alcohol consumption were more likely to have been the victim of a sexual assault.[8] Also common is "date rape."

Over 100,000 American teenagers and young adults travel to resort areas throughout Mexico over spring break each year.[10]

Even more alarming is that students *die* during spring break. Every single year.

There's also a new danger involved in spring break. With videotaping technology being inexpensive, easy to handle and download, "what happens on spring break" doesn't necessarily "*stay* on spring break." Most commonly, young women and teen girls are finding themselves videotaped and exposed on the Internet weeks and months after the partying has long settled into a fuzzy memory. Typically it's a young man or teen boy on the other side of the camera, but according to USAToday.com, professional video crews are paid up to $1,000 a day to entice girls—often at spring-break parties—to show their breasts in exchange for nothing more than a T-shirt.[9]

Finally, though some teens may be aware of international laws that may affect them, most teens and/or young adults are not. For example, while Mexico is known for its beautiful beaches and tropical resorts, and has quickly become among the favorite places to travel during spring break, the country has stiff laws and penalties for breaking those laws, even toward the "young innocents" who were there to party and spend their parents' money.

But parents and teens should beware. An arrest or accident in Mexico can result in a difficult legal situation, often leading to expenses not planned for. Mexican law can impose harsh penalties for violations that would be considered minor in the United States, and U.S. citizenship in no way exempts one from full prosecution under the Mexican criminal justice system.[11] In Mexico, anyone over age sixteen is tried as an adult.

Some domestic locations offer specific safety tips. Daytona Beach and other favorite American spring-break locations warn against drinking too much, offer rules to ward off sexual offenses, and even give a listing of places to "crash."[12]

A Student's Definition of Spring Break

I came across an interesting blog-type Web site where teens and young adults can write their definitions to words pertinent to their lives. Words like *babagalou,* which means "stupid, pointless, and dumb" when defining homework or "retarded but hot" when defining a girl who isn't doing so well in the brains department but charts high in looks.

So, while perusing this enlightening site where you can also write sentences to help better explain the definition, I came upon the words *spring break.* I discovered what kids today are saying about this established rite of passage. Care to read a few of them with me? Oh, and I'm leaving out the bad words, by the way, and correcting the rather poor spelling.

Florida became the focus of spring break in the 1970s. Warm weather, beautiful beaches, and alcohol meant that somebody was going to get naked.... [In the '90s] the presence of so many television and video cameras during spring break meant two things ... somebody was going to get naked, and somebody else would [complain] about it.[13]

Definitions:

1. A weeklong recess from the confines of rigid college life. Many students participate in such acts as: heavy drinking, pot smoking, having sex, tanning on various beaches, and generally passing out. These are often done with a large group of friends who all want to party hard and have a good time, while simultaneously erasing all memories of academia and all-night study attempts from their lives. Many blackmail pictures ensue from this weeklong trip, relationships dissolve, and grades slip another notch.

2. A small vacation where you don't have school for a week in spring, usually in March or April. Spring break is famous because high schoolers and people in college often use this time to go to someplace warm, such as Florida or Cancun, and go wild and crazy, with lots of sex and beer.

3. A ritual event that takes place anywhere from late March to early April. The participants are high school and college students; both of these strange creatures engage in a variety of activities to drive any memories of the school year from their minds. Activities include, but are not limited to: dancing on tables, getting laid, getting stoned and/or drunk, partying, dancing, and staying home and doing absolutely nothing at all. Some tragic consequences can result from this dangerous but important rite of passage, including your girl- or boyfriend finding out you cheated [on] them with eight other boys/girls, your parents finding out how much of an animal you really are, throwing up, getting pregnant, getting raped, and getting killed.

Sentences:

- Marie was grateful for a break from college. She went to the beach for spring break, and ended up getting drunk and having sex.
- Dude, during spring break I, like, got drunk twice, stoned once, and had sex seven times!
- I found out my girl had hooked up with four other guys over spring break, and I knew it was over.

Are There Really Alternatives?

Should church youth groups offer spring-break alternatives? What about parents? Should they allow teens to participate in spring-break activities, thinking their children will not be a part of the debauchery? Do Christian teens fall prey to the temptations of spring break?

The answer to the last question, first. Yes. Yes, they do. And is it any wonder?

I remember when, years ago, a good friend and her husband were heading out for a weeklong vacation. Before I go any further, I should tell you that said friend and hubby were solid citizens within the community and devout members of their church. Yet, as I helped her pack her suitcase, she declared with utter abandon, "I'm so excited to get away for a while. I'm going to throw caution to the wind and do whatever my little heart desires. Eat what I want to eat. Drink what I want to drink. I'm going to just go a little wild." Then she tossed her long dark hair as if to say, "And don't you dare challenge me on this."

I wish I could tell you that she's the first and only Christian adult I've heard take on such an attitude. She's not. If as adults we have a difficult time maintaining our walk during "break," how can we expect our children to do the same?

> While discussing spring-break issues, my husband said, "We all know why the guys are there. The question is, why are the girls there?" I said to one of my daughters after watching MTV spring-break specials, "If I have to see two more girls kissing, I'm going to throw up." She replied, "They're only doing that to impress the guys." I asked Jessica, "Is this the way it really is?" She chuckled. "Yeah, Mother. That's the way it really is."
>
> —Eva Marie Everson

You may be saying, "But I've never done anything like that!" That's good, but *your* teens watch more than *just you,* and they are looking for any excuse.

In a quick poll of Christian teens, we found that—across the board—they knew of other Christian teens who have thrown caution to the wind and become a part of spring break. That said, it's time to look at a few alternatives.

CHURCH ALTERNATIVES

Writer, speaker, and teen leader Robi Lipscomb and I had a lengthy conversation on the subject of church alternatives. "It's easier for churches to come up with spring-break alternatives when the teens aren't of driving age yet. Really, there are plenty of activities," she said. "But it takes a creative youth director to get the older teens." Robi went on to say that spring break is "really no different than summer break, in terms of getting the teens active and keeping them active."

Spring break can be an excellent time for churches to get their youth involved in domestic/international missions or community needs, as well as the typical trips to theme parks, the beach, Christian concerts, camps, etc.

PARENTAL ALTERNATIVE

"Parents don't have a clue," Robi went on to say, "how *really* crazy spring break can be."

Spring break is not the time to attempt to establish relationships with your teen, but rather to strengthen an existing relationship. "If your relationship is strained," Robi said, "find a mentor for your child, someone who can bring accountability to their lives, especially during spring break."

If you and your teen have a good relationship, spring break is an excellent time to do things together. Ask your teen, "What are you most interested in doing?" Then do it. "Parents have to come out of their comfort zone," Robi continues. "Put yourself aside, and let your teen decide. Then you go along."

Attempt to make the time together about growing closer. That said, don't do things like go to the movies or other activities where you are forced to sit and be quiet. If your teen is active in the youth ministry of your church, get involved as well. Again, this should not just occur out-of-the-blue. Your involvement with your teen's group should have been well established by this point.

THE RITE OF PASSAGE

Spring break *is* a rite of passage. But you can help your teen make it a healthy one by playing into it. At set ages (for example twelve and sixteen, or thirteen and eighteen), have an event set aside just for your teen. Do this by telling your child a few years earlier that you plan to do something special—just the two of you. Ask your child what they might like to do. Then help your child plan for it, whether that means travel brochures, choosing an itinerary, or cutting out photos and sticking them on the refrigerator. For example, if your child wants to go ice fishing, you'd cut out some magazine photos of ice fishing, and then spend some time together planning the financial side of things.

For parents with tight budgets, help your child to pick something special but within monetary reality. For example, what if your daughter says, "I'd love to go stay at a nice hotel, lie out by the pool, order room service, see how the other half lives." It's likely that you can find a hotel that offers special packages. Then begin putting away your nickels and dimes. For example, skip one cup of Starbucks a week for one year, and you've got nearly $210.

Above all, make the rite of passage *about your child.* Set everything aside for him or her, and you'll build memories that'll last a lifetime.

JESSICA'S Q & A BLOG

According to news reports and magazine articles, spring break— whether high school or college—is a pretty wild time.

NOW YOU TELL ME: ARE THEY EXAGGERATING, OR HAS IT GOTTEN OUT OF HAND?

James (seventeen, Florida): Living near a beach, I know for a fact that there are giant drunken mobs called parties in allies, wet T-shirt contests, and every form of crazy that drugs and alcohol can bring during spring break. They are not exaggerating, but whether this is called "out of hand" or just fun, I don't know.

Jill (eighteen, Virginia): Spring break is supposed to let off the illusion of parent-free vacationing for teens. Because of the paranoia of the press there is a heightened state of alarm about the time. As long as teens are smart enough to stay away from the "trouble areas," such as out of the country places known for different rules and guidelines from our own, it can be a fun and freeing time. The biggest problem is when teens go out just to try things that are illegal in the States. A prime example is alcohol. Because of the availably of the substance at such places, teens tend to overdo it, leading to drunkenness at best. As long as the person is mature enough to handle the substance responsibly, there shouldn't be any problem with its consumption.

WHAT ARE THE ALTERNATIVES FOR CHRISTIAN TEENS?

James: Every spring break there are Christian beach parties with live bands and games and yelling, all the fun but with God as the aphrodisiac instead of alcohol. If teens want to throw inhibition to the wind, they should use that to witness to people at these events, by talking to them and by showing their enthusiasm the same way they would at a wet T-shirt contest. As lame as it sounds, God's blessing really will give you a greater high than all the drugs and sex of your average secular party.

Jill: You must know yourself and what your limitations or temptations are. If you know you have a weakness in a certain area and don't want to face that, find a group of people you can trust and let the rest come to your better judgment. Always be with at least one other person, preferably someone who knows you well enough to help you out in trouble spots. Just remember your body's and your spirit's limitations before making any definite plans.

Lesa: (youth pastor with more than twenty years in youth work, mother of two teens and one twentysomething): Wow. Spring break. We don't really have an alternative, although now that you mention it, that would be an excellent idea. We have discussed camping trips, mountain retreats, or even short mission trips. Anything to still get away, but keep the kids together in a more wholesome, chaperoned atmosphere.

AS A HIGH SCHOOL TEACHER, WHAT DO YOU HEAR FROM STUDENTS CONCERNING SPRING BREAK?

Brittany (high school teacher and twentysomething woman): Most students look forward to sleeping in and doing absolutely nothing, but the seniors are interested in planning a road trip to the nearest beach. College spring breaks are more notorious, but the seeds are planted in high school for many students.

As a Christian adult, what alternatives would you suggest for parents who want their children to enjoy spring break without the danger?

Brittany: My advice to parents of juniors or seniors is to be proactive in planning a vacation for your kids and their closest friends. If possible take your child and two or three of his or her friends to the beach for a few nights. Stay in a suite to give them some privacy. Give them basic ground rules, but give them some autonomy, too. If your child feels you already trust him, he will most likely live up to that expectation. However, if you treat your child as if she is about to go wild, she most likely will.

CHAPTER 5

Sex, Lies, and the Prom

Or, The Time of My Life

We cannot continue letting the teen magazine editors, movie and television producers, popular musicians and kids' peers determine morality and be the primary influencers of American culture. You people deserve straight talk and clear direction rather than mixed messages and low expectations. It is not enough to tell teenagers to "negotiate" with their dates about the sexual limits before prom. Advice about "safer sex" and warnings against health consequences are a poor substitute for a frank discussion about the psychological and moral consequences of an adolescent's choices. It is time for adults to speak truth to teens. It is time to take back the prom, time to protect our teens and restore their dreams of romantic "promise."

—JANICE SHAW CROUSE, PhD,
"PROM PROMISCUITIES"

W hat is the prom, exactly?

Is it a dance? An over-exaggerated boy/girl party? Is it more about the girl or the guy? Is it about bringing high school to a romantic end? Saying hello to college? Or is it about saying good-bye to sweethearts? Making new sweethearts? Is it about the dinner before or the hanging out at IHOP afterward? Is it a girl buying a dress and a guy renting a tux? Is it about spending enough money in one night that— if put to better use—could be used to feed a small third-world country?

Is it about staying sober? Getting drunk? Getting laid? "Giving it up" for the first time? The last time?

AN AFFAIR TO REMEMBER?

The truth is no matter how many young people you ask "What is prom all about?" you'll receive at least one of those answers. For your high school teen attending prom, there is a plethora of Internet sites where they can read up on all the prom dos and don'ts, including sites that suggest that they can have sex "play" but not sex, if they so choose. Sex "play" is defined as any voluntary sexual activity with or without a partner. Hmmm.

Obviously, for the Christian parent, this is not an option. What we want our children to take away from prom is *not*

- the memory of *being* raped
- the memory of *having* raped
- the memory of giving it up for the first time
- the memory of giving it up for the last time (with that one partner)
- the memory of being carted off to jail for trashing a hotel room
- an unplanned, change-the-rest-of-your-life baby
- an unplanned, change-the-rest-of-your-life STD

What we *do* want for our children is

- the memory of all the preparations
- the memory of the way she looked in her dress
- the memory of the way he looked in his tux
- the memory of having chosen the perfect date
- the memory of the dinner
- the memory of one special dance
- the memory of six crazy kids in the back of one stretch limo

■ the memory of hitting a pancake shop afterwards …
or one of the parent's kitchens where Mom and Dad
had a breakfast fit for kings and queens waiting

TALKING TO YOUR HIGH SCHOOL TEEN ABOUT PROM

Mom and Dad, this could be one of the most bonding events of your teen's four-year high school experience if you will allow it to be. Prom night can truly be an affair to remember, but as parents you must grasp today's reality and talk to your teens. Give them good reasons *not* to have sex on prom night.

TELL YOUR SONS AND DAUGHTERS: DON'T LET YOUR DATE PLAY MIND GAMES WITH YOU.

Sex is *not* expected on prom night. Not everyone is doing it. No one will die—physically or from embarrassment—if you choose abstinence on prom night.

TELL YOUR SONS AND DAUGHTERS: DRINKING WILL NOT MAKE YOU READY.

True, drinking will loosen you up, set your inhibitions free. People will say and do things when drinking that they'd never think to do otherwise. And the rate of drinking among teens is rising.[2] Tell your child, "If it takes drinking to get you to have sex, then your date is not having sex with the *real* you." Everyone wants to be liked or loved or even loved *on* for who they really are. Reality is a big thing right now. (Think reality TV.) Remind your teen that drinking will only add to the misery later. (See end of chapter: Survival Tips for the Parents of Prom-Goers.)

TELL YOUR SONS AND DAUGHTERS TO TAKE A SERIOUS LOOK AT THE AGE OF THEIR PROM DATE.

These are the teen years, and they're supposed to be fun and exciting, full of memories to last a lifetime. Say to your teen, "But if this one night makes a baby, do you really think this sixteen/seventeen/eighteen-year-old girl/boy will be the one to stand up and take responsibility for the next eighteen-plus years?" Remind them of their current age, then say to them, "Think of everything that has happened to you in your lifetime. Everything. Think of every day, every week, every month and every year. Do you want to take care of someone else who is totally dependent on you for another lifetime?"

There are several questions parents should ask their kids regarding any party they want to attend:
1. Will there be parents there?
2. Who will be there?
3. Will there be alcohol?
4. Will there be drugs? Smoking?
5. Can I have the phone number of the parents? (Then call the parents!)
6. Will you call me when you're leaving?[3]

—Janet Holm McHenry, parent, high school teacher, author

TELL YOUR SONS AND DAUGHTERS THAT SEX IS NOT REQUIRED TO FOLLOW "A DINNER AND A DANCE."

Sex will not make the date, the experience, or the memory more special or more complete. Sex will not make you more grown or mature. Only having enough self-control will.

ENCOURAGE YOUR SONS AND DAUGHTERS TO TALK TO THEIR PROM DATE ABOUT THIS BEFOREHAND.

Hey, if this is someone they'd be willing to have sex *with* at the prom, this should be someone they're equally comfortable discussing *not* having sex with before the prom as well. Right?

The Fairy Tale: Prom for Daughters

Parents, this really can be one of the most enchanting nights in your daughter's life. It doesn't have to end on a sour note or leave her with negative memories or even a little "care package." It can end with a sweet kiss good night rather than a trip to the local emergency room or rape clinic.

Begin by helping her *way* in advance to find the perfect dress. In fact, make a day of it. Tell your daughter, "We'll go out for lunch, and then shop for your prom dress." As a special note to single moms and other mothers on a tight budget, don't fret. Lunch can be inexpensive and so can the dress. If you can't afford the monster-priced dress, take your daughter into a nearby town or city and shop re-sale. You don't want her to show up wearing the dress from a classmate's last year's prom collection, so this excursion should help take care of that. Or if you sew or know an expert seamstress, go that route. Final idea: borrow from a friend or relative from another school. It doesn't have to be the most expensive dress, but make sure it looks nice on your daughter.

When choosing a dress, go by quality, not price. Check every seam and every inch of the hem. Remember, your daughter will be dancing in this creation, so make certain she has good movement. Make sure your daughter tries the dress on. Just because she wears a particular size in a "regular" dress, doesn't mean she will wear that size in a formal gown.

Shoes are another issue. What may look like a million may feel like a rock. Make sure the shoes are made for dancing. Also, suggest to your daughter that her shoes not be worn the first time on prom night.

Don't forget to have your daughter order a boutonniere (the guy's version of a corsage, typically one bud, worn in the buttonhole of his lapel) for her prom date.

On the day of prom, give her a day of pampering. Have her nails and hair done, perhaps a facial or even a waxing. Again, if you are financially strapped, you can still do this. Nails can be "press-on" purchased at Wal-Mart or Target. Facials and waxing can be done at home, too. Your daughter's hair doesn't have to be done at the most expensive salon in town, but it does have to be appropriate for dancing. Don't try something new *the day of.* Experiment well in advance.

Another thought is to gather a group of like-minded moms and find out what everyone's expertise is. Maybe one of the mothers is a nail tech or a hairdresser. Make a day of it as a group of mothers and daughters. And don't forget the camera.

Helping your daughter in the "princess for a day and evening" department will also help her to see herself in the way God sees her. Remind her of this. She is *his princess.* She should expect to be treated with respect in every way, this day and every day for the rest of her life.

> Many boys think they're paying big bucks for the "right" to have sex with the girl they're taking to prom. Some parents wrongly think prom night is a rite of passage—that sex is the inevitable course. I know of parents who've paid for the hotel room and sexy underwear. I also know these parents are still dealing with their kids' messed up lives a decade later.
>
> —Janet Holm McHenry, parent, high school teacher, and author of twenty books, including *Prayer Changes Teens: How to Parent from Your Knees*

THE BEST DATE OF YOUR LIFE, WITHOUT THE SEX: PROM FOR SONS

Because so many teen boys talk about having sex on prom, it will be your job as a father or mother to teach your sons differently. This can be the best date of their entire lives, and sex doesn't have to be a part of the equation.

While you're having *that* talk, lend a hand to your son in making this evening spectacular for him, too! Help him pick a suit or tux that best fits his body type.

- Tall, thin prom-going boys can wear any type of suit or tux. Go with a broad-shouldered classic tux or contemporary, single-breasted/four-button suit. Since he's tall, make sure the pants and sleeves are long enough.
- Short and slim boys should not wear double-breasted jackets no matter how cool your son thinks they are. Single-line button jackets with a low-button stance are best. Pants can be classic or pleated, but either way make sure the fit is picture perfect.
- Short and broad sons should wear single-breasted jackets, vests instead of cummerbunds, and dark colors rather than light, since dark slenderizes—something girls have known since fashion first became fashion. Avoid European styles, and keep the look streamlined.
- Tall and muscular or tall and husky young men should avoid anything with frills, anything that adds bulk. If your son is thick in the middle, then like "short and broad" go with a vest rather than a cummerbund. No tails or light colors. If your son is an athlete or otherwise muscular, check the neck of his shirt for a comfortable fit.

Just as with the girls and their dresses, remember your sons will be dancing in these clothes, so make sure that while they look good, they are conducive for dancing.

Next, the corsage. If your son asks you if the whole flower thing is necessary, give him a "duh" look and then smile—because you don't think he's dumb—and say, "Yeah. Yes. Absolutely. You do *not* want to attempt this evening without the flowers."

Your son will need to ask his date *well in advance* about the color of her dress so the florist can best prepare the corsage for her. You'll then want to ask if she prefers pin-on (note: pin-ons are not good for strapless or spaghetti-strap gowns), a nosegay (classically precious, but then she has to carry it around all evening), or the most popular wrist corsage. Encourage your son not to wait until the last minute to take care of this detail. Florists are overwhelmed during prom, and the last thing he wants is to be forced to stop at the local grocery store and hope he can find something fresh in the flower cooler.

Help your son choose a nice cologne for the evening, something that won't overpower the girl but will keep him smelling like the suave gentleman he *will be all evening.* This is also a good time for the "no sex" plug. Finally, make sure he doesn't forget the deodorant.

Of course none of this will happen if your son doesn't actually ask a date. Remind him not to wait until three days before prom. (I'm grinning here.)

You can also encourage your son to be creative. Rather than just picking up the phone, why not help him come up with some romantic or fun way to ask, "Will you be my prom date?" A balloon bouquet with an invitation attached? A floral bouquet? Cards slipped into her locker numbered 1-2-3, etc., each one saying one word: 1=Will, 2=You, 3=Honor, 4=Me, etc. If your son and his date have an ongoing relationship, perhaps her parents can be a part of the fun. If your son and his girlfriend are sports fans, perhaps he can ask her at a sports event or have the invitation written on the marquee of a sporting store. The ideas are endless. Again, this will help your son make prom about romance and dancing, not dancing and sex.

Finally, you'll want to help your son budget. The total cost can be astronomical, but with a little budgeting and a lot of wisdom, it doesn't have to be.

To be considered:

The Tux: Unlike the girl's dress, tuxes can be inexpensive when rented. If your son goes the suit route—even if you spend a little more—he'll get to keep the suit for other occasions.

The Corsage: It doesn't have to be elaborate, just appropriate.

The Ride: If your son decides to go with the expense of a limo, he'll have to decide whether to do this with a group or for just the two of them. A group is cheaper and lessens the chances of after-dance hanky-panky. But he'll also want to tip the driver. As alternate ideas, perhaps the cool parents can trade off with a mini-van ride. Or he can take his own car. Make sure, though, that it's clean and has plenty of gas.

The Haircut: Your son's haircut should not be scheduled for the day of the prom but a week or two before.

Dinner: Things to consider here are:

- Just the two of them, or with a group?
- Reservations and confirmations
- Fun or fancy?
- Don't forget the tip

Photos: Both the guy and the gal may purchase professional photos taken at the prom. If you're a little shutterbug, don't forget to have your camera armed and ready. Batteries are new, film is good, that kind of thing.

After Prom: After prom can include a group going to the pancake house, but can also include more creative outlets such as after-prom limo or helicopter rides. If you live near water, consider a riverboat tour. If you live in a city with nightlife, the possibilities are endless. Some parents may want to offer a "safe place" where the teens can come for after-prom socializing.

SURVIVAL TIPS FOR THE PARENTS OF PROM-GOERS

While this night will make you glow with pride, cost you a small fortune (or at least feel like a small fortune), and be an event filled with picture taking, once those little-ones-all-grown-up drive away toward the dance, you'll no doubt begin to worry. Here are some tips for *your* survival.

- *Communication is key*. Know your teen's plan for the *entire* evening.
- *Communication is key*. Talk to the other parents and the school officials.
- *Communication is key*. Find out if any of the other parents are planning to be part of the event or if they are offering after-prom activities. Take shifts doing prom-duty, but avoid *embarrassing* your child.
- *Communication is key*. Ask your teen's school what the prom rules are and the consequences for breaking them. Go over these rules with your teen. Give a list of your boundaries and the consequences for breaking those, too.
- *Communication is key*. If your son or daughter is heading to prom in a limo, find out about the alcohol policy of the limo company. Do *not* assume anything. Remember, alcohol plays a huge part in prom sex.

JESSICA'S Q & A BLOG

NOW YOU TELL ME: HOW EXPECTED IS SEX ON PROM NIGHT?

Erin (high school teacher and parent): I would say it is pretty much expected that sex will take place on prom night, especially if kids have been dating for some time and haven't engaged in it yet.

Unfortunately many parents enable their children to engage in sex, drugs, etc., on prom night by renting rooms and having parties where drinking is taking place. It is too easy to have kids wander off, and too hard to monitor if your own judgment is impaired. These are not poor inner-city kids; these are the upper-middle suburban kids I am talking about, although the problem was the same when I worked in inner-city Houston.

WHAT ADVICE WOULD YOU GIVE PARENTS ABOUT PROM NIGHT? WHAT CAN PARENTS DO TO HELP THEIR TEENS MAKE PROM AN EVENING TO REMEMBER RATHER THAN A NIGHT TO REGRET?

Erin: *1. Care*—too many parents don't. This is the one night above all others you should want to be involved in planning.

2. Don't treat prom like a wedding—limos, expensive dresses, and tuxes induce romance. Prom should be romantic, but they aren't getting married. Set limits on what will be spent on prom. Prom is part of a long-honored tradition meant to introduce young adults and debutantes into society. It is the old-fashioned ball where classy men and women were put on display. If kids understand this, they are less likely to treat it as a dress rehearsal for the wedding night. Prom is to introduce the cream of the crop in class—so let your children know they need to be classy and keep their pants on.

3. Don't ever trust—this is a sad thing to say, but kids need to have boundaries. I was the kind of child who said one thing and did another—and I was the president of my church youth group as well as a state rep for my church. My mother was strict, but she let up around prom and graduation, because she wanted to give me the benefit of the doubt and treat me like an adult. Seniors are *not* adults. Know where they are at all times that night, and don't be afraid to drop in or call them on their cell phone. Make sure they are home at a reasonable hour; don't bend the rules because it's prom night.

4. Get involved—schools always need prom chaperones. Be one. Also, suggest after-prom parties that are impressive and well chaperoned. Rent out theaters, putt-putt courses, or create activities in your school with prizes no one wants to miss. Believe me, businesses will get involved! If no one is doing it, then you get it started.

5. Talk to your kids about sex—don't be shy. Kids need to know that you know what's up. Explain to them that you know they are going to want to have sex and that prom night sets the tone. Tell them you understand what "the heat is on" means and that it isn't just an expression; saying no is one of the hardest things they will ever have to do. Explain your expectations and what the consequences will be if they do have sex. Tell them you will be asking them if they had sex the next day, and let them know you will expect an answer. Some kids are less likely to be tempted if they know they will have to lie outright.

6. Reading/Roles—there is a book for girls titled *He's Just Not That Into You*[4] by Greg Behrendt and Liz Tuccillo. It is phenomenal in teaching girls how to know the way boys think about sex. My husband always says boys are "predators" (and we have no girls), and while I think that's a bit strong, I do understand boys are wired differently. Teach girls that in many cases they have to be the ones to say no. Most boys will take what they are offered or allowed to take, and if the girl allows it, they will think she is okay with it … and thus, since they have feelings for one another, it is morally okay as well. Religion and morality sort of get tossed out the window when it comes to sex; it feels like there are exceptions to rules when the lights are down and the blood is flowing.

7. Tell boys what it really means to be a man—the media makes it look like to be a man is to be sexually active. A real man, one who is most attractive to a girl or woman, is one who treats her with honor, who will not pursue her sexually even if she seems to invite it. I am aware that in these times, many girls are tossing it out there for boys. Let boys understand that they are the leaders; God intended them to be men, to define what will be acceptable for their households when they are grown. Would they want their future wives to think sex outside of marriage, even their own marriage, is acceptable? Doesn't that set things up for infidelity later? Do they want their (future) daughters to be sexually active?

OKAY, THIS IS FOR THE TEENS. DID YOU ATTEND A PRIVATE SCHOOL OR PUBLIC? WHAT CAN YOU TELL ME ABOUT PROM THAT YOU THINK PARENTS SHOULD KNOW?

Katie (eighteen, Pennsylvania): I did attend a small private school (about twenty-five students in grades 9–12). I, along with my mom, planned the prom. It was not allowed to be associated with the school due to religious differences, so it was held on the rooftop at a local hotel. I think parents should know that prom is a great experience for students. You get to see everyone you usually see, only they have taken the time to clean up. The guys go the extra mile to look good, and the girls love to dress up.

Prom doesn't have to be about sex or drinking. You can go and have a good time without either of those. I felt no pressure about sex with prom. That may be because I attended such a small school; I knew the guys there, and I knew they had morals. I can't say what it is like at a public high school prom, but at our prom, there was no pressure. Most people came as friends, not dates (which is a great way to spend prom). You don't have to worry about how or what your date is doing, and you can go have a good time. I think parents just need to talk to their kids about prom. Make them know that not everyone is "doing it," and that they shouldn't feel pressure. Prom is about having a good time with friends, not stressing out!

CHAPTER 6

Sex, Lies, and Dating 101

Or, Where Are You Going, My Little One, Little One?

Dating can be a wonderful experience—one that allows us to grow and mature in our understanding of and relationships with the opposite sex. Dating gives us opportunities to learn how to relate, communicate, and deal with the sometimes difficult issues that arise between girls and guys. Done right, dating can be purposeful, fun, and a blessing. Done wrong, it can be a drain and a distraction from God's purpose for us.

—KAROL, GRACE, AND JOY LADD,
THE POWER OF A POSITIVE TEEN

You can double-date at fifteen," my parents informed me as a young teenager. "You can single date at sixteen. You can do things with the church group and your friends before that, but you'll have a strict curfew."

Good basic plan. Alas, enter reality.

When I was fourteen years old, I went on a church missions trip with a few of the other churches in the county. With vanloads of kids heading toward the South Carolina border, I ended up sitting next to a fine young man named Robbin.

Robbin was about to be a high school senior. I was about to be a freshman. We snoozed the first part of the trip, then talked like old friends when the sun rose over the eastern sky. As a matter of fact, we talked the entire weekend. We talked, and we talked, and we talked.

And he kissed me. Kissed me right there in the middle of a church missions trip.

When we arrived back to our hometown, Robbin drove me home. He came in, spoke with my parents (*such a good ol' Southern boy!*). My mother fed him cake still warm from the oven. She poured him a glass of milk. When he asked for permission to take me out, my mother quickly replied that we'd need to stay with a group. I wasn't quite fifteen yet, but I would be soon, and that at fifteen we'd talk about anything else.

At the Savage household, we gave our teens the option of not dating at all. In grade school we used the term game to define boy-girl relationships at that stage of their lives. We told them that other kids in their grade would play the "boyfriend-girlfriend game" but that they wouldn't play it at such a young age. As they entered junior high and high school, we began to talk about the possibility of dating, but we included the option of not playing the game at all until they were old enough to be looking for a life partner.[2]

—Jill Savage, Got Teens?

Long story short: Before my fifteenth birthday I was "single-dating" Robbin. He was a complete gentleman throughout the entire nine months of our courtship. But when we broke up and I was still fifteen, it seemed silly to say that I couldn't single date the next guy who came along.

And the next guy who came along wasn't such a gentleman. He was daring and sexy and, like James Dean, a rebel without a cause. Dating, for me, would never be the same.

The History of Dating

If you've read our first book, *Sex, Lies, and the Media* (Cook Communications, 2005), you know that what constitutes dating today—whether for teens or adults—wasn't always the way of things. About a hundred years ago, a young man knocked on a young lady's front door when he wanted to spend time with her and then counted his blessings that he got to sit in the front parlor with her and the rest of her family. "Courting candles" were lit. When these small candles burned out, it was time for the young man to go home. No need for Papa or Mama to say a word.

During the Depression, when large families often shared small living spaces, "dating" outside the house became both preferred and acceptable. Life was difficult enough, and finding an escape via amusements helped ease the agony of reality.[1]

Where would they go? Often, to the movies. During the post–World War II era, we began to see a change in the types of movies produced, as producers shifted their target from the family market to the thirty-and-under market. Then, in the 1950s, as teens dominated the American landscape, the focus of dating changed. It was no longer about finding that perfect someone with whom you could spend the rest of your life. It was about having a good time, which every teenager figured he or she deserved. And most parents of those teens wanted something better for their children than the Great Depression they had endured.

Things have kept on changing. What we have today doesn't begin to come close to the old idea of two young people courting because they desire to build a future together. What we have today is all about fun and games.

SINGLE-DATING/DOUBLE-DATING/GROUP-DATING IDEAS

Whether or not you allow your teen to double date or single date is obviously up to you. Group dates are the safest, but what your teens decide to do once they get with the group is up to them. (We'll talk about this more later.)

What teens can do on dates within a city varies greatly from what they can do in smaller towns. What has always amazed me, though, is that no matter *where* teens live, I hear the same old thing: "It's so boring here." With everything at their fingertips, our teens are bored. The "dinner and a movie" routine may not be good enough anymore. Movies often portray sexual images, which leads to sexual temptations and feelings.

So our teens have been forced to become creative. As one young man said to me, "We keep our dates active and planned."

I talked with a few teens and asked what they do—whether small town or big city—to keep their dates real, fun, and sexually safe. They say one key is to think of dating ideas for daytime rather than nighttime. Here are a few of their suggestions, all of which can be done single, double, or in a group setting:

- Get a canvas and some paints, then go to a park (public) and paint. Finger paint, throw the paint. Whatever. Get two canvases, and paint something for each other. Then you get a souvenir of your date.
- Go to museums and art galleries.
- Find less common out-of-the-way places, like theme restaurants.
- Spend an afternoon at a bookstore. Coffee and a good book ... or journaling together.
- One mom told me about her son and his girlfriend who took a personal DVD player, went out for Chinese take-out, then went to a park in the middle of the day, spread a blanket, ate Chinese, and watched a DVD.
- Take pottery or ceramic classes together.
- Share common hobbies, like photography.
- Participate in or watch sports.
- Go to a supervised home for movies.
- Attend church-sponsored events.
- Go bowling, skating, etc.
- Get tickets to the opera, the symphony, a concert, or a play.
- Hold adult-supervised parties.
- Join a teen club together.
- Play laser tag.

WHEN YOUR TEEN IS MADLY IN LOVE

Bradley and Abigail (names have been changed) fell in love nearly the minute they laid eyes on each other. He was wearing dark slacks and a crisp white short-sleeved shirt. She was wearing a pretty dress with smocking across the bodice. She remembers his dimples. He remembers her curls.

They were six years old and in first grade. It was Bradley's good fortune to have Abigail sitting right in front of him and—even at such a young age—he now recalls that her hair always smelled good. Two weeks later, with just enough education to scribble, Bradley slipped a note up to Abigail:

I lik you. Do you lik me?

Abigail turned slightly in her seat and smiled at the blushing boy sitting behind her. He held his breath for what seemed to be an eternity, and then she nodded. Bradley exhaled and smiled, displaying a gap where he'd lost his two front teeth just days earlier in a tumble with his big brother.

Throughout that year and all the elementary school years that followed, Bradley and Abigail could be seen about campus during recess and lunch, holding hands, giggling, talking, and passing notes in the hallway (when they were placed in separate classrooms at their parents' insistence). Though they developed strong relationships with others and were active in sports, social functions, such as Girl Scouts and Boy Scouts, and church, they still had eyes only for each other.

Elementary school gave way to junior high and junior high to high school. Nothing changed for Brad and Ab (as they were now called) except for their physical bodies and, of course, a strong desire for each other. By this time their parents had come together and worked out a plan to keep their children pure, allowing for the input of the little lovebirds but not letting it be the deciding factor. Brad and Ab stayed grounded in the Word, in youth groups, typically dated within group settings or doubling with good friends. They planned diligently to keep their dates in public settings, like walk-in movies, football games, city softball, and youth group outings.

Eventually, high school graduation arrived, gold tassels moved from one side of their caps to the other, and Brad and Ab began to prepare for separate colleges. Four years and two diplomas later, Bradley and Abigail (as they were once again called) married.

Bradley and Abigail's story is rare, of course, though it is not unusual to hear of high school sweethearts dating for the four years of high school or even of young couples meeting during high school and marrying later. When or if this should occur, however, parents need to have a new set of rules to help maintain purity between their children. The first rule, however, is for the parents: Remember that the physical attraction between your son and his girlfriend or your daughter and her boyfriend is extremely powerful and potent and that—as best the young people can ascertain—they are in love!

No matter how dedicated to the Lord and the Lord's work these teens may be, they are still susceptible to falling into each other's arms in a weak, passionate moment. In fact, the more they talk about the deeply intimate spiritual issues of God, the more apt they may be to become sexually active with each other. Our relationship with God is designed to be such a magnificent, personal, mind-blowing thing, it mirrors the emotions involved with healthy, married sex. (Don't forget who created sex in the first place.) Many a strong, church-going, Bible-thumping, missions-supporting adult has fallen into sexual sin with someone equally as spiritual. It would be foolish for us to imagine that our children wouldn't have the same temptations.

For this reason—if for no other—guard the dating life of your in-love teens carefully. Be careful of the seemingly harmless things they do together—like exercising together, homework, and, yes, even Bible study. If they are going to study the Word together, it should be in a public room—not a bedroom—with the doors wide open and perhaps with an adult leading them. What a beautiful thing to imagine: teaching a possible in-law the Word of the Lord.

Set boundaries of no single dating. Though it seems the most obvious two people to single date are those who are "in love" or who have a long-standing relationship, this is sexual activity begging to happen. Tell your teens no, but explain why. Then help them to come up with other dating ideas. Note: Nothing can keep your teens from slipping off together once they get with a group of people, but your disapproval will—at the least—add to the discomfort factor.

If both parents or both sets of parents work outside the home, be aware of the dangerous after-school hours. Ask neighbors to do check-ups. Let your teens know that even though the house is unoccupied of adult bodies, adult eyes will still be watching.

If you have an agreement between the teens that allows for him to pick her up before an evening out with the gang, etc., and then to bring her home, stress "no car time." Meaning: As soon as you enter the car, you exit the driveway. As soon as you enter the driveway, you exit the car.

As they become closer, keep all conversations about marriage to a minimum. These conversations, which include romantically fantasiz-ing about days of wedded bliss, will eventually lead to talking about sex. The more it gets talked about, the more they will try to rational-ize going ahead and doing it.

Equally as important is helping them understand who they are apart from each other. Their identity should not be found in each other, but in Christ first, then in themselves. Ask your teen, "If this relation-ship doesn't work out, what will you do? Where will you be? Who will you be?"

I have strong feelings on this. No human being should be depend-ent solely on another. I remember well a couple from my high school days who were so wrapped up in each other they dropped all other rela-tionships. Within a short period of time, their love story became a nightmare. With the relationship in an unhealthy state, they broke up but were emotionally scarred. I also know married couples who make their lives solely with each other. Outside of the two of them, they have no life.

Parents have been known to do that with their children, too. In the first case, when the other spouse leaves this earth, what will the surviving spouse do? In the second, when the child moves on to college, marriage, and their own parenthood, what will the parent be left with but emptiness?

While they may not understand your motives entirely, your nearly grown children will respect you and—years later—honor you for your wisdom. This isn't, after all, about keeping something wonderful away from them, but more about saving it for the proper time.

Your Child, Your Choice

This discussion carries with it a series of questions whose answers vary from family to family. When do you allow your teen to start dating? Should you set up a standard and stick to it, or see what happens as it happens? Can you judge the dating time of one child by another? Should you be alone in the process or make your teen a part of it? Is it about age, really, or about maturity? Why do teens date? Is it really necessary to the whole *teen experience?* Do teens date because of peer pressure and popularity issues or simply to have someone to do things with?

One Child Versus Another

There is no value or wisdom in comparing one child to another. We all know enough stories from our personal pasts or the pasts of friends to know that having the same DNA does not mean having the same personalities, goals, boundaries, skills, and temptations.

When, Where, and Who?

Asking a group of ten parents or youth workers when a teen should begin dating will give you about the same number of answers. I know. I tried it. Some say it depends on the maturity of the child. Others say sixteen, while others say no dating at all.

There are enough books and articles out there to thoroughly confuse an already confusing issue, and we won't add to them. Well, okay. We will. Each child *is* different, but you must at least have a boundary to work with. Then you have to factor in everything else. Personality. History. Location. And who the "date-ee" is.

I remember the afternoon I received a phone call from high school bad-boy Neil Lewis (not his real name). My mother answered, called me to the phone, and gave me a distinct look. You know, the one that raises an eyebrow and says, "Just what is *this* all about, young lady?"

I took the phone from her hand, said hello, then swallowed hard.

"Hey, this is Neil," the young man said.

"Hi, Neil," I answered, trying hard to demonstrate the love of Christ in spite of feeling a bit unnerved by the call.

"Just wanted to see if you'd like to go to the movies with me tomorrow night."

> When their friends no longer have faces, you're in trouble.[3]
>
> —JLP, member of Narcotics Anonymous

I ran my fingertips through my hair and struggled for an answer. My time spent dating the "rebel without a cause" had left me pretty wise on what path this date could lead me down. "Well," I said, chipper as I could be, "I'll have to ask my mother. You understand. Southern mother and all." I looked over at my mother, who was ironing laundry but keeping one eye and ear pointed in my direction. Her lips had formed such a thin line, they'd nearly disappeared.

"Oh, well, sure," he said. "I understand."

I placed my hand over the phone, asked my mother the question I already knew the answer to, and moments later returned to my phone-suitor. "Neil?" I began. "My mother says we have plans tomorrow night." It may have been watching television, I don't remember, but the answer was "No, sir!"

The point I want to make is twofold. 1) Even as a "seasoned dater," I asked my parents for permission to go out. Many teens today go out on dates, informing their mothers and fathers as they walk out the door of what their plans are, rather than asking for permission. If permission is not required, this is a mistake on the part of parents. 2) My parents made the final decision on all dates and on the locations of the dates. "Where are you going?" "Who will be there?" and "What will you be doing?" might have caused me to roll my eyes, but in the end I knew they loved me enough to ask.

So, what do you do about the child who refuses to be straight with you? Or the one who refuses to live within the boundaries you set for dating?

I went to a few experts in the field with this question only to discover they'd never raised a child who was dead-set on doing things his way. And while Jessica's memories of her high school dating days may be far different from her father's and mine, I'm here to testify to you that Jessica was one of *those teens*.

I can only remember a handful of times her dates actually came to the house. Jessica was more apt to go out with a group of people, most of whom we never saw. I can think of only one time that Jessica came to us and asked for permission to go out with a young man, but by that point she was at least eighteen.

There is a vast difference in your child going out with teens you know versus those you don't know. And since I had no clue as to what I was doing—so how could I honestly advise you?—I asked some of my wise friends what they had to say on the issue. I was thrilled when they reminded me that even though Jessica didn't always adhere to the rules, she turned out to be a fine young woman.

Here's their bit of wisdom salted with hard-earned experience, followed by Jessica's two cents' worth. Read these words carefully; they may be the only advice you'll *ever* get on this subject.

> **Tracy writes:** I had to kick my young teen son out of
> the house. It was painful, but [would have been] more

painful if he stayed. He struggled, and that was hard watching him. Now, a few years later, he is studying to be an evangelist and is guest preaching/teaching at his church and developing a radio ministry. So, even with the evils out there, kicking them out where they have to fly on their own may not necessarily be wrong for some kids. I still grieve over it, but thank God for all he did for the entire situation.

Two things that helped me tremendously—I read Stormie Omartian's book *The Power of a Praying Parent*[4] so many times I practically memorized it. I used specific prayers in the book to pray them over my son as he went through a variety of difficult situations. He still had to leave, and still went through heck and back, but I believe the prayers were answered in God's time, not my own. Also, I prayed, and continue to pray, Ephesians 6:11–18 over him—the full armor of God. I see the difference it makes.

Ron writes: Our sixteen-year-old daughter (now happily married and producer of our adorable grandson) was supposed to be friends with a boy in the youth group. They were supposed to date only in a group. They went to church activities, our house, his family's house, etc. One day my wife found a note in our daughter's bedroom that she had written her friend, and it detailed what they had been up to—and it wasn't good. My wife called me; we felt like we had been punched in the stomach.

My wife then called our daughter's boss at work and explained that she would be leaving for the day. I picked her up from work (during her shift), brought her home, and we had a long talk with her. She screamed at us, "You hate me!" My reply: "We have loved you every day of your life."

We called the boy's parents and went over and met with them and their son and explained our concerns. Namely, that the boy (along with our daughter) knew our family rules, but disobeyed them. We asked that he stay away from our daughter.

We explained to our daughter how she had broken our trust and that now she had a new best friend to hang out with (her mother). We took away her freedom for the summer, when she continued to contact him or maybe he contacted her—I think we took away her phone, computer privileges, car keys, etc. … As she said: "I have no life."

We explained that because she was underage she could live at home and obey us—or live at juvenile hall. Those were her two choices. When the boy continued to contact her—we told our daughter if she didn't put a stop to it we would call the police and get a restraining order against him. Our daughter was a very unhappy camper—but after a few months she began to see the light.

When her Mr. Right came along—a few years later, he called our house and asked my permission to take our daughter out. He did everything above and beyond what a parent could ask for. He wrote her beautiful love letters. He married her. And she is so thankful that we intervened.

Carol writes: I remember the days. I just know that I prayed a lot, and to this day our daughter still mentions it:

"Mom, I bet you were really praying hard."

"You better believe it, sweetheart."

At that stage they need us to trust them. Also, can they trust us? It goes both ways. That's where the faith comes in. You meet your teen halfway, come to an

agreement, and then pray, pray, pray while they're
away, away, away. And when they come home, meet
them with a smile, a hug, and no questions about
details. No nagging.

If they break the trust, the lesson will be: If you
are old enough to make a promise, you are old enough
to keep it. How will you keep the promise inherent in
a contract signed when you get a job? Marry? Borrow
something meant to be returned? It's about integrity.
Honesty. Being accountable, faithful, and all that.
Words they're not always interested in.

I also think there's a huge place for a non-family
mentor with these teens. More than likely they will be
willing to listen and to open up to someone other than
parents.

Deb writes: Concede that you can't and won't physically force them to obey your rules, but make sure they
understand that your rules are tied to privileges. If they
don't obey rules, they get no allowance, no use of the
car, no cell phone or computer access, etc. Sure, they'll
just get a ride with friends, but at least you aren't fund-
ing their behavior. Parents can make teens pretty
uncomfortable merely by not providing the niceties
teens have come to take for granted. Few teens, even
with full-time jobs, can pay for all those extras on their
own, so those become your bargaining chip.

If things really get tense, arrange for your teen to
live temporarily with a friend or relative. With our
oldest daughter, it was the idea of being under our
authority that chafed. She was an angel with all other
authority we placed her under—teachers, youth leaders, grandparents, etc. Her problem was only with us.
She's twenty-five now, in her third year of teaching,
happily married, and expecting their first baby. She

and her husband are youth leaders and active in their
church. To this day she doesn't know why she bucked
our authority so strongly and doesn't think there's anything we could have done differently. We just had to
ride out the storm. By the time she was a junior in
high school, things were much better, and we could
trust her judgment and give her enough freedom that
she no longer felt the need to rebel.

With our youngest son (also now a sweet, well-
adjusted college grad) there was a point (in eighth
grade) where we saw him headed the wrong direction with a bad crowd. After an incident with the
police, we forbade him to hang out with those kids
except at school and church, and we threatened to
put him in a military school if things didn't improve.
That may sound overly dramatic, but we were dead
serious, and he knew it. We had the school picked
out and everything.

We told him we were not going to allow him to
disrupt our entire family and set a terrible example for
his siblings. It scared him into submission, and he tells
us now that it was a turning point for him. (Also, our
kids attended public school, and we often told them
that if we saw they couldn't handle the pressures of
public school, we would happily do whatever necessary
to afford a private Christian school education for
them, which would mean leaving behind friends and
everything familiar. That threat also served us well.)

I guess the bottom line is that after a certain age,
we can't (legally, anyway) physically control our kids.
All we can do is make sure we keep them as safe as
possible and don't condone their rebellion or make it
overly easy by financing it with cars, cell phones, com-
puters, fancy bedrooms, and other perks that seem to
reward bad behavior.

Teresa writes: I don't think there is any way someone else can give advice in this area. Without
knowing the child, it would just be a shot in the
dark. Having said that, I will say that removing
money, privileges, cell phone, etc., has usually
worked at my house. My oldest son just became a
father. We had many rounds with him over curfew
and other things. As he held his newborn in his arms
I couldn't help myself; I asked him what he was
going to do when she didn't come home until four
in the morning. He looked at me and said, "You've
been waiting a long time to say that to me, haven't
you?" He was right.

JESSICA'S BLOG

As we were writing this chapter I asked a handful of grown-ups if
they thought dating was essential to the teen experience. They all
agreed that it was, and for several reasons. For one, they felt that
not dating would cause more curiosity about the dating experience. Most of them recalled that the kids (especially the girls) they
knew growing up who were very restricted or who had little freedom, ended up "wild." (And not in a good way.) One friend even
likened it to three horses being set free for the first time. Two had
never left the stable and the other frequently went out into the cor-
ral, under his owner's supervision, to roam.

After being released, one of the confined horses ran off so far
he was never found again. The second horse refused to leave the
barn. The latter continued to graze out a few feet farther and
returned before the sun went down.

While there is certainly danger in the world, there is also a
danger in not allowing your children to grow apart from you.

Children, as they become teens, will scream to become their own people. This means, for the parent, allowing them "outside the barn" as they are ready.

Valuable social skills are acquired and honed during this time. It would be more beneficial and safer for teens to learn some of the initial lessons while still under their parents' care and watch.

KEEPING IT SAFE

DATE RAPE

One of the last things a parent thinks about as he or she watches a daughter slipping through the doorway with a date is the possibility that the young man guiding her toward his car could actually rape her before the evening is over. For parents of a daughter, there is no fear quite like the one that reminds you of your daughter's vulnerability.

The same goes for the parents of the boy. Nowhere in their wildest imaginings could they create a scenario where their precious little son could physically force a girl to have sex with him.

And yet it happens. All the time.

As responsible parents who talk to their sons and daughters about sex and sexuality, the topic of rape and date rape is a must-do. We *must* educate and direct our sons to respect a young woman, and we *must* teach our daughters how to avoid the dangers, recognize the signs of endangerment, take steps to protect themselves, and know what to do in the case of rape.

First, let's define date rape. Date rape (also known as "acquaintance rape") occurs when a boyfriend or male friend forces his "date" to have sex or unwillingly participate in sexual activity of any kind. Though dating is a natural and exciting part of growing up and helps with further development of social skills teens will need as they become adults, date rape is *not* natural. In fact, we'll go one step further and say that *sex* should never, ever be an expected part of the dating experience. No matter what media says.

Here are some facts about this issue that every parent must know.

- Though most dates never lead to violence, parents should take the time to talk about date-rape prevention *before* their teen begins dating.
- When people think of rape, they might think of a stranger jumping out of a shadowy place and sexually attacking someone. But it's not only strangers who rape. Twenty-eight percent of women and young women who are raped are raped by their boyfriends; 35 percent by acquaintances.
- Date rape is one of the least reported crimes.
- Women who are raped during the course of a date are four times more likely to be between the ages of sixteen and twenty-four.
- Eighty-four percent know their attacker.
- Ninety percent of date rapes include drinking.[5]
- Though females are most often the victims of rape, it can happen to guys, too.[6]
- Even if a couple has been intimate or nearly intimate before, no means no. Young women should know their choices (although yes/no/yes is not a game) and young men should learn to respect the decision of the girl. If he feels she's playing a game, he must be in control enough to simply drive her home.
- Rape involves forced sex, yes, but it in no way is about love or passion. Rape—date rape or otherwise—is an act of aggression, violence, and control.

Parents, we must teach our sons and daughters about healthy, godly relationships with the opposite sex. While we are teaching them about God's will for their bodies (pure love) and their sexuality, we must also teach them that *true love* involves respect. Teach your daughters that if a date, friend, or boyfriend is pressuring her to be intimate, that's not a healthy relationship. Similarly, we must teach our sons that sex is not something one person *owes* another, and that someone who *really* cares will show respect to another's wishes and not apply force or pressure about sex.

DATE RAPE PREVENTION

Moms and dads, when you sit down and have that talk with your daughter, you might want to say:

Daughter, if your date ever ...

- gets hostile when you say no;
- ignores your wishes, opinions, and/or ideas;
- attempts to make you feel guilty or accuses you of being uptight if you say no to sex;
- makes light of your conviction to God's will for your body and your life;
- tries to find loopholes in your commitment to a contract or vow;
- acts excessively jealous or possessive;
- keeps tabs on your whereabouts; or
- displays destructive anger and aggression ...

... talk to us. No one—neither one of us—will accuse you of wrongdoing. We will calmly listen to what you have to say and help you right the situation. If you need strength in breaking off the relationship, we are there for you. If you need us to come get you, we will without hesitation. Our primary goal is to keep you safe and to raise you to be the woman of God you were born to be. You are our princess. More than that, you are God's.

Jessica's Blog

To Your Daughter: A lot of times date rape could be avoided by being careful where you find yourself on a date. You don't want to end up alone or in an impassioned and compromising situation. In general, we girls need to be responsible for the situations we put guys in. Whether or not our intentions are to lead him on, the more physical we allow things to become, the more likely something undesirable could happen.

To Your Son: It's just as important for a boy to be aware of a girl's reputation as it is for a girl to be aware of a boy's. Guys, if a girl is known as a tease, you'd do better to stay away from her. That's your protection.

The following is a collection of tips to share with your daughter:

Protecting Yourself from Date Rape

- Know that it could happen to you. It can also happen to both males and females.
- Date someone you know well, not someone you hope to know better.
- Until you get to know someone well, stick to group dating. Drive your own car so you have a way home if necessary. There is nothing wrong with meeting him there.
- Blind dates should never be taken alone—no matter how well your best friend knows the guy.
- Never, ever, ever go off with someone you barely know. Seeing someone in a group setting even for several weeks doesn't mean you *know* him.
- Be assertive in setting boundaries for relationships. Define your limits by saying just how much even a

male *friend* can touch you. Even a kiss on the cheek or a brotherly hug is a boundary that can be crossed.

- Remember, a guy who never gets to first base has less of a chance of getting to second and third.
- Know in advance what your boundaries will be. Don't make them up as you go along.
- If a date wants to take you to a place where you think you will be uncomfortable, don't be afraid to speak up. Be ready with another choice. If he continues to pressure you, be ready to ask to be taken home or to call your parents.
- Avoid the "dirty talk" guy. Again, this is one boundary that should never be crossed. In fact, you'll need this boundary time and again as you reach adulthood and the working world.
- Equally as important is to be careful of the young man who tries to impress with gifts—especially expensive ones—too soon in the relationship.
- Prepare yourself for the fact that not all young men will take "no" like a gentleman. But remember you are not responsible for *his* reactions, only your own.
- Sad to say, but true to research, most date rapists are men who conform to traditional, rigid sex roles. Therefore, it is important to know a young man's views toward sexism to prevent rape.
- Always go out with plenty of cash. Make sure your cell phone is fully charged. Use that cell phone to call home periodically. If you are faithful in this, your parents will know instinctively if something is wrong.
- Have phone codes with friends. Make sure someone knows where you are at all times.
- Stay aware of the situation and circumstances around you. If you are at a party and the lights dim or the music turns sensual, this could be a potential danger.
- Stay sober. Alcohol and drugs alter a young woman's

and young man's judgment. Just because he decides to drink or do drugs does not mean you have to stick around to see the results. (This is when the money you brought will come in handy.)

■ Pay attention to your beverage. It should come directly from your server if you are in a restaurant or sports event. If you are at a party, insist that you can get your own drink. If you are drinking from a glass, bottle, or can and are in a crowd, keep your hand or thumb over the opening.

■ Never leave your drink unattended, or even attended with a good friend. Never share a drink. If you *do* leave your drink unattended and return to find it looks different, has been topped-off, or just have a strange feeling about it ... throw it out.

> Rohypnol is now being reported as being one of the "in" drugs on high school and college campuses, and particularly in college fraternities.[7]
>
> —Clark Staten

"Bad beverages" don't have to be alcoholic. Though date-rape drugs can increase the potency of alcoholic beverages, they can just as easily be slipped into soft drinks, coffee, tea, etc.

■ If you suddenly, for no explainable reason, feel drunk or even slightly incapacitated, get to a safe place or speak to a "safe person," like a friend or an adult you feel you can trust.

ROOFIES, ECSTASY, AND GHB

Rohypnol—also known as "roofies," "ruffies," "roche," and "rope" (as well as by a few other names)—is the most popular date-rape drug, so-called because many young girls who have unknowingly ingested it (Rohypnol is easily ground into a powder and slipped into a drink) have woken up alone, undressed, dazed, and confused, and yet keenly aware that they have been sexually assaulted. Because it is cheap ($2.00–$4.00 per pill street value), it is considered the "love drug of choice."

Rohypnol is a brand name for *flunitrazepam* and is a Benzodiazepine prescription (like Valium, though ten times stronger). Its medical use is as a preoperative anesthetic or strong sleeping pill. Usage of the drug began in Europe in the 1970s, and it was first seen in the United States in the early 1990s. It has been considered an illegal drug since 1996.

Strong doses of Rohypnol can bring on amnesia. It is tasteless and odorless, though when mixed with alcohol it can give a drink a bitter flavor. If placed in a light-colored drink, Rohypnol will change the color of the drink to blue.

The effects of Rohypnol are:

- bloodshot eyes
- slurred speech
- slowing of psychomotor skills (no coordination)
- muscle relaxation/a sedative effect
- amnesia

When combined with alcohol or marijuana, health risks increase. Together they can suppress the central nervous and respiratory system, causing respiratory depression, seizures, aspiration, liver failure, coma, and even death. The effects of Rohypnol are felt within about ten minutes after ingestion and reach their peak within eight hours. All traces of the drug disappear within twenty-four hours, making legal prosecution difficult.

Ecstasy

Also known as "E" and "love doves" (as well as by "X" or "XTC"), Ecstasy is another name for methylene-dioxymethamphetamine

(MDMA). It was originally used to reduce appetite, but the recreational use of the drug was introduced in the early 1980s.

MDMA acts on a brain chemical called serotonin, a neurotransmitter that transfers messages across the synapses (or gaps) between adjacent neurons (nerve cells). Serotonin is thought to play an important part in shaping mood, thought processes, sleeping patterns, eating patterns, reaction to external stimuli, and control of motor activity.[8]

The effects of Ecstasy are

- chills
- "wiggling" eyes
- blurred vision
- heart palpitations and an exhilarating rush
- dry mouth
- hot and clammy skin
- stomach churning
- occasional hallucinations
- lights seem brighter, sounds seem louder, touch becomes more sensitive, everything seems lovable

Side effects include strain on the heart, liver, and kidneys. The body can dehydrate quickly and overheat.

Users of Ecstasy begin to feel the effects within twenty minutes, but the effects last from three to ten hours. Inhibitions are loosened and users experience an emotional bond with people around them—even people they just met or don't really know. They feel good about themselves overall.

Unlike Rohypnol, Ecstasy can be detected in the urine for two to four days. Taking Ecstasy can be fatal. Those who have died from it have had temperatures as high as 110 degrees due to the body overheating.

GHB

Also known as Liquid Ecstasy, Blue Nitro, Midnight Blue (as well as by other names), GHB (gammahydroxybutyrate) has become popular with the party scene. Users enjoy an alcohol-type high. Sexual side effects are potent.

GHB releases dopamine in the brain, causing users to simply relax or to fall asleep, even when given low dosages. It comes in a liquid form and is nearly tasteless.

The effects of GHB are:

- the loss of inhibitions
- exhilaration
- relaxation

Side effects of GHB are disorientation, nausea, muscle spasms, numbing of the muscles, and vomiting. It takes anywhere from ten minutes to an hour to take effect. When used as a date rape drug, one in five victims surveyed in a June 2000 report said they could not remember the assault. Seventy percent said they were unable to resist the assault after being slipped the drug.[9]

> Oh, my goodness. Middle school kids are the worst right now. They're experimenting with sex right in the middle of the schools.[10]
>
> —Dr. G. W. (Bill) Reynolds III

IN-SCHOOL ASSAULTS

According to the Department of Justice, over 19,000 in-school (inside school buildings or on school property) rapes occurred in this country in 1999, which is 10 percent of all rapes reported. Approximately twelve thousand in-school assaults were reported in 1994. If this doesn't shock you, see if you can grab ahold of this statistic on WorldNetDaily: SESAME (Survivors of Educator

Sexual Abuse and Misconduct Emerge) released a survey of high school graduates in which they stated that 17.7 percent of male students and 82.2 percent of female students reported being harassed sexually by school faculty or staff; 13.5 percent reported actually engaging in sexual intercourse with a teacher.[11]

If Your Daughter (or Son) Is Sexually Assaulted

While it is understood that you should never make your child feel as though he or she has done anything to deserve being sexually assaulted, it is just as important to report the crime. While this may be as painful as the actual assault, you can help your child to release a false sense of guilt, but at the same time help him or her be honest about the circumstances.

Get immediate medical treatment for your daughter or son.

Get *good* counseling. Note: When a young man is the victim, a different scope of emotions surface. But just like a daughter, your son will need your support.

Above all, remind them how precious they are and always will be in God's sight and in yours.

CHAPTER 7

Sex, Lies, STDs, and Pregnancy

Or, When Fears Become Reality

Usually when I am concerned about something in our kids' relational life or have a gut feeling that something is wrong, I am right on the money. We parents should ask the hard questions so often that hearing them becomes normal.

—JILL SAVAGE AND PAM FARREL, *GOT TEENS?*

Do you know what I've just loved about writing this book? Discovering that I'm not alone. Not as a parent nor as a once-upon-a-long-time-ago teenager.

Okay, so here's what I've discovered (although I wasn't too shocked): Teens are having sex. Even Christian teens. Books are being published, articles are being written, parents' knees are hitting the floor, and every day Christian teens are finding themselves (as we used to say) "in a pickle." So rather than gloss over this part of the book with a now-we-know-this-could-never-happen-to-you attitude, we're going to spend a little time getting real. We may as well. Satan has sold our teens—our *children*—a pack of lies. It's time we do what we can to combat those lies. We start by telling the truth.

DESIROUS ONE PLUS DESIRED ONE CAN EQUAL AN UNWANTED THREE

There are two unwanted physical consequences for your teens when they engage in sexual activity: an STD and a pregnancy.

STDs

Every year three million teens—about one in four sexually active teens—get a sexually transmitted disease (STD, also known as STI, or sexually transmitted infection, and once known as VD or venereal disease).[1]

The number is nearly overwhelming. By the age of twenty-one, one in five Americans requires treatment for an STD.[2] (In fact, American teens have the highest rate of STDs *in the world*.) Two-thirds of those who contract an STD will be under the age of twenty-five.[3]

Chlamydia is more common among *teens* than among older men and women.[4] *Teens* have higher rates of gonorrhea than do sexually active men and women aged twenty to forty-four.[5] Some studies show that up to 15 percent of sexually active teenage women are infected with the human papillomavirus (HPV), many with the type of HPV that is linked to cervical cancer.[6]

One thing that as a parent you will want to stress to your teen is that STDs do not stay within the boundaries of social/economic lines, racial divides, religious affiliations, or gender. *Anyone* of any age who is having sex *can* get a sexually transmitted disease.

> Despite signs that things are improving, the reality of sexual temptation remains—and Christian young people are not inoculated against these pressures.[7]
>
> —Jennifer Parker

STDs are more than just a tear on the fabric of your family. They are a serious health problem. It left untreated, permanent damage can lead to infertility (between 100,000 and 150,000 women become infertile each year as a result of STDs[8]), mental and emotional problems, and even death.

Over twenty-five STDs are commonly reported and at least eight new STDs (including HIV/AIDS) have been identified since 1980.[9]

Five of the top ten exportable infectious diseases in 1997 were STDs, including the top four (chlamydia, gonorrhea, HIV, and syphilis).[10] Keeping that in mind, let's begin with a look at the top four.

CHLAMYDIA[11]

Sometimes called silent (because a person can have it but not know it), chlamydia is a curable sexually transmitted disease. It can cause serious problems in men and women (such as penile discharge and infertility, respectively), as well as in newborn babies of infected mothers. Early symptoms may be mild and easily confused with gonorrhea. Chlamydia is treated with antibiotics. However, many patients are never treated because they are unaware that they have been infected.

> Chlamydia, America's most common sexually transmitted disease, is most often seen in teens and young adults, report CDC researchers. Teen girls had the highest number of cases.[12]
>
> —Miranda Hitti

About four million cases of chlamydia are reported every year in the United States.[13] Because the cervix (opening to the uterus) of teenage girls and young women is not fully matured, they are at particularly high risk for infection.

Symptoms and Treatment

If your daughter complains of an abnormal vaginal discharge or burning sensation when urinating, and you suspect or know that she is sexually active, she may have chlamydia. Some individuals have lower abdominal pain, low back pain, nausea, fever, pain during intercourse, or bleeding between menstrual periods. However, the disease can spread from the cervix to the fallopian tubes and still be asymptomatic. Chlamydia can spread from the cervix to the rectum.

If your son complains of discharge from his penis or burning sensation when urinating or has burning and itching around the opening of the penis, and you suspect or know that he is sexually active, he may have chlamydia.

Chlamydia can also be found in the throats of those who have had oral sex with an infected partner. With oral sex being popular among teens today as a means of *not* having sexual intercourse, this is an even greater possibility for them.

Chlamydia can be cured with antibiotics.

GONORRHEA[14]

It seems that gonorrhea has been around forever. Years ago it was called "the clap." It is among the most common, curable STDs and is caused by a bacterium called *Neisseria gonorrhoeae.* It grows easily within the warmth of the reproductive tract.

Gonorrhea can be passed from one person to another through vaginal, oral, or anal sex, even when the infected person has no symptoms. It also can be passed from mother to baby during birth. You *cannot* catch gonorrhea from a towel, a doorknob, or a toilet seat.[15] However—and this is important—ejaculation does not have to occur for gonorrhea to be transmitted or acquired. It also is possible to get gonorrhea more than once.

> The risk of pelvic inflammatory disease (PID) is as much as ten times greater for fifteen-year-old females than for twenty-four-year-old females. PID can cause sterility.[16]
>
> —L. Westrom

Like chlamydia, the symptoms are not always easily detected. They usually begin anywhere from two to ten days and even up to thirty days after having sex with an infected partner. Left untreated, it can lead to PID (pelvic inflammatory disease).

Symptoms and Treatment

In the female, symptoms are often mild. But if your daughter complains of a burning sensation when urinating, or increased vaginal discharge, and/or vaginal bleeding between periods, and you suspect or know that she is sexually active, she may be infected with gonorrhea. Symptoms are often mistaken for simple bladder or urinary tract infections.

If your son complains of a burning sensation when urinating, or a white, yellow, or green discharge from his penis, and you suspect or know that he is sexually active, he may have been infected with gonorrhea. Sometimes infections cause swollen testicles.

Because it is not unusual to find that patients with gonorrhea also have chlamydia, both tests are usually run in the same visit. Like chlamydia, gonorrhea is treated with antibiotics. However, drug-resistant strains of gonorrhea are increasing in many areas of the world, including the United States, and successful treatment of gonorrhea is becoming more difficult.

HIV/AIDS[17]

Probably no STD in the history of sexual desire has caused fear in the hearts of mankind like HIV/AIDS. HIV stands for human immunodeficiency virus, and it causes AIDS, acquired immunodeficiency syndrome. AIDS was first reported in the United States in 1981 and has since become a major worldwide epidemic.[18] More than 830,000 cases of AIDS have been reported in the United States. It is estimated that as many as 950,000 Americans may be infected with HIV, one-quarter of whom are unaware of the infection.[19]

When a person becomes infected with HIV, the body's immune system is damaged and unable to fight infections and certain cancers. Once a patient is diagnosed with AIDS, he or she may get life-threatening diseases caused by common and ordinary viruses or bacteria that would not affect a healthy person.

HIV is contracted by an infected person passing on his or her sexual fluids or blood to another. The most common way is by having sexual intercourse, but a person can also become infected by sharing needles or by receiving contaminated blood from a transfusion—though few cases have been reported—from an infected person. Mothers infected with the disease can pass it to their unborn children.

Symptoms and Treatment

If your son or daughter becomes infected with the HIV virus, they may be asymptomatic for a month or longer. Many people first complain of flu-like symptoms, and the disease is often mistaken for a viral infection. This is dangerous, because it is during this period that the infected person is most infectious and HIV is present in large quantities in genital fluids.

Though silent (for some people, up to ten years), the disease is rapidly spreading, infecting and killing cells of the immune system. Those who have been infected eventually begin to complain of fatigue; weight loss; diarrhea; frequent fevers and sweats; thrush; persistent yeast infections; persistent skin rashes; PID that does not respond to treatment; swollen lymph nodes of the neck, armpits, and groin; and short-term memory loss.

HIV is a big problem for young people, as well as adults. In 2004, it is estimated that there were 2.2 million people under [the age of] fifteen living with HIV.[20]

The most effective treatment for HIV is highly active antiretroviral therapy, known as HAART. HAART is a combination of several antiretroviral medications that aims to control the amount of virus in an infected patient's body. It is also important to keep the overall immune system healthy.

Currently there is no cure for AIDS.

SYPHILIS[21]

Syphilis is an STD that, at one time, was responsible for devastating epidemics. According to a November 1, 2002, press release from the CDC (Centers for Disease Control and Prevention), despite continued declines among African Americans and women of all races, overall rates of primary and secondary syphilis have increased slightly for the first time in more than a decade.[22]

Syphilis, which is sometimes called "the great imitator" because its early symptoms are similar to those of many other diseases, is an STD marked by long duration or frequent recurrence and is highly infectious. Though it begins in the mucous membranes, it quickly spreads in the bloodstream.

Symptoms and Treatment

If untreated, syphilis will go through four stages:

1. *Primary.* Painless ulcers called chancres occur on the genitalia, anus, fingers, lips, tongue, tonsils, or eyelids. Females may develop chancres on the cervix or vaginal wall. The chancres usually heal after three to six weeks even when untreated.

2. *Secondary.* Begins within a few days or up to eight weeks after the ulcers appear. Symptoms include headache, nausea, vomiting, fatigue, appetite and weight loss, sore throat, and slight fever. A rash can occur on arms, palms, soles, face, and scalp. Drainage that occurs from this rash is highly contagious. Some people experience hair loss.

3. *Latent.* In the latent stage, physical signs and symptoms are usually absent, although the rash may recur.

4. *Late.* Symptoms depend on which organs the disease has invaded. If it has invaded the nervous system, headache, dizziness, sleeplessness, seizures, and psychosis may develop. Lesions may occur on the skin, bones, or any body organ. These lesions are usually painless but can be disfiguring. Syphilis can also affect the heart and kidneys.

Syphilis can be spread from a mother to her unborn baby during pregnancy, but getting it from a blood transfusion is rare, as the bacteria dies after ninety-six hours in stored blood.

Syphilis is easily cured with penicillin in the early stages. Treating syphilis once does not protect you from getting it again.

OTHERS STDS[23]

When I was in my single years, I never really thought about the risks I was taking. Getting pregnant wasn't an issue; I was on the pill. I just didn't think about diseases. Until I got one. Treatable, not curable. So, I dealt with it. Then I had to tell the man who would one day be my husband, hoping he wouldn't leave on account of it. And then, worse still, I prayed for nine straight months that my unborn child would not be born during an outbreak. All that for a few minutes of "pleasure."

—From an anonymous conversation with the author.

Before we continue talking about STDs, allow us to encourage you to contact your community health department, family physician, or take extensive time to do your own research on the Internet. Then sit down with your teens and talk intelligently about the disease risks—both short- and long-term—involved with having premarital, extramarital, and multipartner sex.

PID (PELVIC INFLAMMATORY DISEASE)

In sexually active women, PID is most likely to occur between the ages of fifteen and twenty-five, and is a chronic infection affecting the uterus, the fallopian tubes, and the nearby structures in the lower abdomen. PID affects more than one million women in this country every year and can cause ectopic pregnancy and infertility.

HSV (HERPES SIMPLEX VIRUS)

In the 1970s you could scarcely swing a bat without hitting someone who had genital herpes. With discos and the moral fiber of the country down the tubes, clinics and doctor's offices were filled with men and women complaining of swollen glands around the groin, discharge, painful urination, fever, headaches, and muscle aches. Eventually they were complaining of sores, blisters, rashes, and severe pain.

And they are still complaining.

One out of five of the total adolescent and adult population is infected with genital herpes. One in five Americans has genital herpes, yet at least 80 percent of those with herpes are unaware they have it.[25]

A major reason for the epidemic proportions of herpes is that anywhere from 10–30 percent of herpes carriers are asymptomatic. They don't show signs of the disease and sometimes don't know they are infected. But they can spread herpes during shedding periods, when the virus is on the surface of the skin, even though they will not have an outbreak.[26]

A lot of myths revolve around this disease. So to be able to talk with your teen about the dangers of herpes, you must first know *truths* rather than what

> About one in five people in the United States over age twelve, which accounts for approximately 45 million individuals, is infected with HSV-2, the virus that causes genital herpes.[24]

someone whispered to you in the locker room during high school PE.

First, herpes is an STD, which is spread from one person to another by oral, anal, or vaginal sex. It is one of the most common types of STDs in the world. A person who contracts genital herpes has it for life. For life. While outbreaks can be treated or even suppressed, the disease is permanent.

There are two types of herpes simplex virus. Type 1 (called HSV-1) and Type 2 (called HSV-2). Genital herpes is typically caused by HSV-2. The usual symptoms of HSV-1 are cold sores in the area of the lips. The usual symptoms of Type 2 are sores in the area of the genitals. Either may be spread by kissing or by sexual contact, including oral sex.[27] You cannot get genital herpes from toilet seats.

People who have genital herpes are more susceptible to HIV.

GENITAL WARTS

Genital warts are caused by *human papillomavirus* (HPV). HPV is the name of a group of viruses that includes more than one hundred different strains or types. More than thirty of these viruses are sexually transmitted.

Low-risk HPV also may cause abnormal pap test results or genital warts. (These are not the same warts as what any person might have on hands.) High-risk HPV may lead to cancers of the cervix, vulva, vagina, anus, or penis. In 2003, 264,000 cases of genital warts were reported to the CDC by doctors' offices.

Genital warts can be treated. A doctor can prescribe medication or remove the warts, but the viral infection remains inside the skin and more outbreaks are possible. Each outbreak must be treated separately.

The preceding in no way expresses the number of possible STDs teens may be exposed to if they are sexually active. You will want to do a personal study to know them all.

In Hosea, God said of his people, "My people are destroyed for lack of knowledge" (Hos. 4:6). Please do not assume *anything* when it comes to your teen. It is imperative that you arm them with knowledge—whether they are sexually active at this time or not.

WHEN THE MERRY-GO-ROUND STOPS

"Mom. Dad. I'm/She's pregnant."

As a parent, can you think of one sentence you don't want to hear more than that one? Let me tell you … if your teen is sexually active, he or she worries about having to say it, too.

With all the information out there concerning protection and even abstinence, teens still get pregnant. Why? For one thing, there is a greater distance between a young girl becoming sexually mature (meaning she is old enough to become pregnant and bear children) and the average nuptial age, which is twenty-five. If the average girl begins menstruating at age twelve and yet she—on average—does not marry for another ten to thirteen years,[29] she will live with increasingly high hormone levels in a modern society that screams sex.

> The average cost of a baby's first year is about $22,000.[28]
>
> —Julie K. Endersbe

The same goes for sons. Whether they are mentally or spiritually ready for sex is not the issue. The fact is, they are physically ready for sex, and yet men are marrying later and later in life. Still, one in every fifteen men fathers a child while he is a teen. Many of these are not named on the child's birth certificate.[30]

Half of all teen pregnancies occur within six months after the female first begins having intercourse.[31] But teen pregnancy isn't just a statistic. When it's happening to your child, it's not a social issue, either. It's a personal problem. In fact, the word *crisis* might better describe it.

It's also a decision—or an endless list of them—to be made. For a moment, you will feel as though you failed as a parent. For a while you might be ashamed of your child or of the situation. Then you will begin to count the costs. All of them. Including the dimes and nickels.

But in a bit you will pray, and the Lord will give you the guidance you seek. You will be able to help your child through one of the most difficult periods of his or her young life. And if your daughter (or the mother of your son's baby) decides to keep the child (or if the couple chooses to marry), you will have a most precious legacy to hold in your arms—a child to introduce to the marvelous stories of Jesus.

GUIDING YOUR TEENS DURING THIS TIME

In the case of teen pregnancy, lives will change. Everyone's life. Even if you, the parent, say to your teen, "I will *not* raise another child," or "This is *your* problem to deal with." Lives—*all* lives involved—will change.

The most obvious choice to make in the beginning is whether or not to keep the baby after birth. (We will not discuss abortion in this book, as we do not believe it to be an option in *any* situation.) Whether going with adoption or choosing to parent a child, teens who face pregnancy will want to take parenting classes and birthing courses.

ADOPTION

Before talking to your teen about adoption, there are issues you will want to be "up on." There are two ways a young woman can go when choosing the adoption route: with an agency or with an attorney. An agency can offer open, semi-open, or closed adoption, as can an attorney. In either case, the birth mother must ask questions. She needs to inquire as to policies and flexibility regarding how open or closed an adoption may be.

An open adoption is "open" communication between birth and adoptive parents and includes frequent access to the child. Birth parents may be included in birthday parties and other events and may be able to visit with the child at times. The birth and adoptive parents set boundaries they are all willing to live with.

Semi-open adoptions maintain confidentiality, but allow adoptive parents and birthparents to exchange pictures

> Of the approximately 2 million pregnancies that occur among unmarried women each year, only 1 percent choose adoption, while 49 percent abort the child and 50 percent choose to parent.[32]
>
> —Linda Rooks

and letters at agreed-upon intervals. Sometimes visitations can be arranged in advance of the placement of the baby. Photos, videos, and even visitation rights are made. Even things like "I really want the baby to have piano lessons" can be expressed with the understanding that those expectations will be met if possible. Birth parents and adoptive parents will meet at least once.

One of the most important options for a birth mother in open or semi-open adoption is that she is able to pick the adoptive parents for her baby. Under certain circumstances, the birth father also can participate in this decision.

> Thirty-five percent of teen girls become pregnant at least once as a teen—850,000 per year.
>
> —TeenPregnancy.org

In both open and semi-open adoptions, the adoptive parents most often pay legal and medical costs. If the birth mother requests counseling to help her cope with placing the child for adoption, this also can be part of the arrangement.

In closed adoptions the birth mother or father may be given some information about the adoptive parents, but has no interaction with them. They will not receive photos or letters. If the birth parents desire to know *something* about the adoptive parents, then a limited amount of information is given.

In all three cases, birth parents can register (though this may vary from state to state) to be contacted by the child after his or her eighteenth birthday, if the child so chooses.

LETTERS OF LOVE

If your daughter or son makes the decision to have a baby placed for adoption, it will be one of the most precious gifts of love he or she can ever bestow. If they choose open or semi-open adoption, encourage them to write a letter to their child, expressing that love and the desires they have for the child. This not only will be a part of the healing process for the birth parent, but also will be of value to the adopted child years down the road. As birth grandparents, you may choose to do the same.

ADOPTION AND TEEN FATHERS

The rights of teen fathers vary from state to state, so if your son learns he is about to become a father, you would be wise to contact an attorney. Today a few states have what is known as "birth father registry," which allows a man to confidentially declare that if the sexual union he is in with a woman results in pregnancy, he must be notified. This allows him the right to decide to raise the child, if he so chooses.

ADOPTION AND GRANDPARENTS

The rights of birth grandparents vary from state to state. To know more about what your state allows, you would want to contact an attorney.

KEEPING THE BABY

If your daughter is pregnant and decides to keep the baby, there are many issues for her to consider. Will she and the father marry? Will she/they continue to live at home? Will she/they get a job to help pay for the expenses? Will she/they need government assistance? Will she/they continue to go to school? How will she/they support the child emotionally and spiritually? If the baby has physical complications, how will she/they cope? How will she/they provide for childcare? Is she/are they willing to give up most of their social activities, friends, and dreams for the future?

First things first. You'll want to help your daughter or son get rid of *all* romantic views of parenting. At the same time, be supportive. Your support is essential. Let them know that they *can* continue to move toward their dreams. Remind them God still loves them. If your church does not spiritually and lovingly support your teen during this time, find another church. Girls and boys who have been kicked out of churches for making a mistake may *never* find their way back in.

Yes, they've made a mistake. A costly one. But Jesus' mercy, grace, and especially his blood are so much greater than this.

JESSICA'S Q & A BLOG

Interview with a birth mother who gave her baby up for adoption:

HOW OLD WERE YOU WHEN YOU GOT PREGNANT? WHAT WERE THE CIRCUMSTANCES?

Kristy: I was twenty. I'd been raised in a solid Christian home. We were in church every Sunday and I was active in youth programs.

> The amazing thing is, teen mothers have no clue. At first it's all about the cute little baby clothes, and then two or three weeks after the birth of the child, they're saying, "What am I going to do?"[33]
>
> —Tricia Goyer, author of *Life Interrupted*

WHAT ABOUT THE FATHER OF YOUR BABY?

He went to church with me but wasn't active before that. We dated for three years before I got pregnant and, before that, had talked about getting married. But when he found out I was pregnant, he said, "This isn't what I wanted."

WHAT HAPPENED NEXT? HOW DID YOU DECIDE ON ADOPTION?

As clichéd as this may sound, I didn't decide. I just asked the Lord, "What do you want, because I'm not capable of making this decision?" It was probably a month after I asked that question that the doctor asked me, "Have you thought of adoption?"

I didn't make the decision right away. I told the doctor I would think about it. I prayed for the next six months. Over the course of three months, I did a lot of soul searching, praying, and waiting, and in the meantime doing the best I could to nurture the baby.

But every time I went into the doctor's office, he asked about the adoption. He said, "I know a Christian couple who would really love to adopt a child." Every time I would leave I would pray, "Lord, if it's your will."

I was in my ninth month. I was out on my parent's porch, and I just got very real with God. I said, "Lord, I can't give this baby up. I love her so much. I'm so bonded. But I keep thinking this is something you want me to do. So if this is your plan, I'm going to ask that you not make me see her."

You see, at that time, in the state where I was living, the birth mother had to physically hand the baby to the attorney. I told the Lord that if I didn't have to see the baby, I'd know for sure.

About three weeks later I got a call from the head of the hospital where I would be giving birth. He said, "The attorney you consulted has brought it to my attention that you might give this child up for adoption."

He said, "The doctor says you don't want to have to see the baby. So, we are going to make allowance, but you will have to sign a waiver giving all rights to the adoptive parents."

As soon as I said yes I would do it, a peace came over me, and I knew God was truly in control. Two or three weeks later I went into labor; my older sister was home from college, and she drove me to the hospital. Then my parents arrived. I had a long, long labor.

What I remember most is that when I went to sign the papers, my mother was there and was told she had to be a witness. She started crying, saying, "I can't give my grandchild up."

I ended up ministering to her. She signed, and we cried together. The nurses were coming in, saying, "Your faith is amazing."

When she was born, I remember looking at the clock when I heard her cry. It was 2:02. But they immediately wrapped her up and took her out of the room, and I never saw her.

To this day I hurt, no doubt about it. I had to go through a process. But God allowed me to grieve for this child. And it hurt. But in the middle of the grief, Jesus was there, and I never felt one ounce of guilt or that I'd done the wrong thing—because I knew she was going to a wonderful home.

I felt like Hannah, who gave her Samuel back to God. She didn't rear him, but she knew she'd done the right thing by giving him to God. For me, I didn't give her to the adoptive parents as much as I gave her to God. Then he gave her to the parents.

God has blessed me with two other beautiful children who love the Lord. Through it all, he did a work in my whole family and in me. He even opened the window of opportunity for me to forgive the father publicly, in my church. It was truly an amazing moment, filled with tears and rejoicing.

Interview with a teen mother who decided to keep her child:

WHAT IS IT LIKE, BEING A TEEN GIRL, AND FINDING OUT THAT YOU'RE PREGNANT?

Tricia: I didn't think it could happen to me. I was worried about my future and what others would think. I hated the thought of my sweet grandparents finding out. I wanted to drop out of life and disappear.

One day I was your typical high school senior. An honor student, a cheerleader, and a yearbook editor. I worked part time at McDonald's to pay for gas for my car and my clothes. The next day, I was a mother-to-be. I knew lots of people who had babies, even a few at my school. I also have to admit I was my own worst enemy. I was lonely and scared. Grumpy and standoffish. I felt like a kid but now had a huge responsibility. Me, a mother?[34]

WHAT CHOICES DID YOU MAKE CONCERNING KEEPING THE CHILD, MARRIAGE, ETC.?

Since I'd previously had an abortion, I was determined to keep my son. My boyfriend and I were on the rocks, and I knew marriage wasn't an option. In fact, I was pretty sure it would be me and this kid for life. The amazing thing is that God brought an amazing man who loves me and my son. It was my pastor's son! We started dating when my son, Cory, was two weeks old, and we got married when Cory was nine months old.

WHAT SUPPORT DID YOUR PARENTS GIVE TO YOU?

My stepdad let me know he would help where he could. My mom was the real trooper. She helped sign me up for continuing education classes. She took me to all my appointments. She was my labor coach and babysat for me so I could attend college classes.

HOW DID THE CHURCH HELP?

I did not want the church involved when I got pregnant, but they wouldn't leave me alone. The pastor's wife (now my mother-in-law) came to our house to pray with me. I turned my back on her, but she just sat there in my room praying. My grandma's Bible study group invited me to their home study. I went because I had nothing else to do. They even threw me a baby shower at church. Their love showed me the love of Jesus!

CHAPTER 8

Sex, Lies, and Abstinence

Or, Just Don't Do It

In the U.S. most people become sexually active eight years before marriage.

—JULIE K. ENDERSBE, *TEEN PREGNANCY*

A ccording to the stats, things are getting better. Fewer and fewer teens (and, again, that includes Christian teens) are having sex.

An August 5, 2005, report from the CDC (MMWR—Morbidity and Mortality Weekly Report)[1] shows that engagement in sexual intercourse in teens between the ages of fifteen and nineteen and who have never been married is—for the most part—decreasing.

In **1995**, 43 percent of boys **fifteen–seventeen** years of age reported having had sexual intercourse.

In **2002**, 31 percent of boys **fifteen–seventeen** years of age reported having had sexual intercourse.

In **1995**, 75 percent of boys **eighteen–nineteen** years of age reported having had sexual intercourse.

In **2002**, 64 percent of boys **eighteen–nineteen** years of age reported having had sexual intercourse.

In **1995**, 38 percent of girls **fifteen–seventeen** years of age reported having had sexual intercourse.

In **2002**, 30 percent of girls **fifteen–seventeen** years of age reported having had sexual intercourse.

In **1995**, 68 percent of girls **eighteen–nineteen** years of age reported having had sexual intercourse.

In **2002**, 69 percent of girls **eighteen–nineteen** years of age reported having had sexual intercourse.[2]

> A lot of the teen years are spent in trial and error. They make a decision, and it's a good one. Another one, not so good. This is one they can't afford to get wrong.
>
> —Eva Marie Everson

With the exception of the last statistic, it all sounds promising. The problem is in one word: *intercourse.* Today's teens have difficulty agreeing on the definition of *sex.*

In our book, *Sex, Lies, and the Media,* we asked a handful of teens if sexual intercourse was the only solid definition of sex, or if other forms of sex (such as oral, digital, anal, etc.) sex were also considered *sex.* Their answers varied. One said, "I've never really known the answer to this, so I'd be interested to hear."

Another said, "Only intercourse is sex."

A final comment was: "These days, kids are, like, 'I'm having oral sex, but it's not sex.' I'm, like, "It's not called oral kissing; it's called oral sex."[3]

Before you can talk openly with your teens about *not* having sex, you'll need to understand the truth about what constitutes sex these days. Be specific with them. Tell them in the most detailed terms—even the ones you aren't so comfortable with—what does and does not constitute sex. Remember how creative *your* generation was at getting around this age-old problem. Know that this generation is even more creative than ever.

Added to the problem is that, more and more, media portrays sex outside of marriage as normal, okay, and expected. The church, on the other hand, is telling them less and less. We are entertaining rather than teaching. Pacifying rather than preaching.

And Satan is watching with a glint in his eye.

DEFINING ABSTINENCE

And what is abstinence, anyway? Is it just the absence of intercourse, or a decision to stay *totally* pure until marriage? Is kissing involved in the rules? Handholding? Heavy petting?

If you ask a handful of teens, you'll get a handful of answers. Many abstinence programs are struggling to find the answers as well. Some encourage abstinence to reduce the number of teen pregnancies and the incidence of STDs among America's youth. Some want to talk about the spiritual consequences. Others are restricted from doing so.

It can be confusing, when it's meant to be anything but.

I took a stroll along a particular Web site with links concerning abstinence in preparation for this part of the book and discovered basically *nothing* about abstinence. I learned about "what the first time feels like" and "how to know when I'm ready." I even learned how to French kiss. But nothing that truly promoted waiting. (There were other Web sites and books that were helpful; we've listed these at the end of the book.)

WHAT'S SO BAD ABOUT JUST NOT DOING IT?

We've been quick to talk to our daughters about self-esteem and even occasionally about self-respect. But we're not so quick to talk to our sons. Perhaps the first step in encouraging abstinence is in helping both sons and daughters understand their own value and the value of others. Yes, if they have sex they could get an STD or get pregnant. But is that the *real* point for Christian parents? What about teaching them, showing them, reminding them how important they are to God, to you, to the other family members, to the community, and especially to themselves?

For God did not give us a spirit of timidity, but a spirit of power, of love and of self-discipline.

—2 Timothy 1:7

I remember hearing the story of a young girl who was being taunted by other girls in her class for being a virgin. (The story could be just as true for boys.) For a while, the girl ignored the taunts. But one day, exhausted by the whole thing, she turned, took a breath, and calmly said, "You are what you are. And I am what I am. I can be what you are any time I want. But you can never be what I am again." This story illustrates one of the best definitions I know of a teen who is *sure* of herself and of her reasons for remaining pure before marriage.

ANOTHER FAVORITE STORY

Another story that made the rounds on the Internet a few years back is of a father who went to a meeting at his son's school where parents would be informed about a new course in sexuality that was to be taught. He arrived and, while he was surprised to find only a handful of other parents there, he began to shuffle through the paperwork concerning the program. STDs and pregnancy were expounded upon, but abstinence was barely mentioned.

He asked why this was and was met with laughter. "Why don't you go back to burying your head in the sand?" someone asked.

But the teacher explained the job of the school was to teach "facts," while the home was the place for giving moral instruction. The father sat quietly and listened to the course being defined and described.

After a period of time, the teacher said, "Doughnuts in the back." Then she added, "Oh, and right next to the doughnuts are nametags. Would you put them on please? And please mingle with the others during this break."

The father remained seated and watched as the others got their nametags and doughnuts, shaking hands as they introduced themselves to one another. Though the teacher encouraged him to join in, the father didn't move.

"The doughnuts are really good," she said.

"No, thank you."

"Well, then. What about a nametag? I'm sure others would like to meet you."

The father shook his head, no.

"Oh, please join them," she continued to encourage.

But the father heard a firm, "Do *not* join the others" from deep in his spirit. "I'll wait here," he reiterated.

Minutes later, the teacher called everyone back together. "Now please pull off your nametag," she said. "We're going to show you something we teach the children." The nametags were peeled away from shirts and blouses and dresses. "On the back of one of the tags," the teacher continued, "I drew a little flower. Who has it?"

"I do," a man said.

"Very good, sir," she said. "Now, class, the flower represents an STD. Who shook hands with this gentleman?"

A few hands went up.

"The handshake represents sex," the teacher said. "So those you shook hands with now have the disease." She turned to those who now had the disease. "And who did you shake hands with?"

Pretty soon it was evident that everyone in the classroom had the disease. All but one. The father's hand went up. When he was acknowledged, he said, "I'm sorry if I caused a bit of an upset earlier. You've done an excellent job at showing us how you will demonstrate to the children about sexual encounters and disease. But there's one little thing I'd like to point out."

"What's that?" the teacher asked.

"Not all of us are infected," he said. "One of us *abstained*."

ESTABLISHING FRIENDSHIP

In the late 1970s when Debby Boone (singer of the hit song "You Light Up My Life" and daughter of famed actor and crooner Pat Boone) was engaged to Gabriel Ferrer, they went on a speaking tour and on national television—on programs such as *The Phil Donahue Show*—declaring their decision to remain pure before marriage in an effort to encourage other couples to do the same.

I remember watching them and hearing one of them say, "This forces us to become friends. And it's friendship that will sustain us throughout our marriage. Sex won't." (That may be a paraphrase, as it's been quite a few years since I watched the show, but it is true to the original content.)

I have repeated this story to my children, primarily because it's true. "Your father and I were friends *long* before we dated," I told them. "And should we ever stop having sex, we'll be friends long after." I told them about how, after a miscarriage followed by a host of medical issues, we were not able to have intercourse. "This didn't crush our marriage," I said. "Our marriage was built on more than sex."

Abstinence *forces* you to become friends. Or to see if you have anything with which to build a friendship. Anyone can feel passion or lust toward another someone. But friendship—true, lifelong friendship—is rare.

Think about it. Most of us have *very few* friendships that have withstood the test of time. The lifelong friendship found in marriage is priceless. It should be able to stand on its own merits and not be governed by sex.

REDEFINING SEX

As we stated earlier, sexual intercourse is on the decrease, but sexual behavior is not. The key phrase is "everything *but!*" So how do we keep our kids' paws off each other in every way, shape, and form? We must first get real enough to talk about all these issues. If words like "oral sex" or "manipulation" (fondling yourself or your partner to the point of orgasm) bother you, then you may want to practice saying them with a best friend ... or your pet goldfish. Teens are not afraid to say these words. Media is not ashamed to say them, show them, and define them.

It's time for us, the parents, to *redefine* sex. To talk about the beauty of married intimacy and how premarital sex can alter that. Be armed with Scripture that speaks about the sexual union between a man and a woman, between the married couple versus the unmarried. Be ready to answer their questions. Be ready to listen.

ARMED WITH INFORMATION

Perhaps before you sit down and have a detailed conversation with your teen (and this talk should have started *years* ago, by the way) about abstinence, it would be a good idea to have information at your fingertips to show them. Finding photos on the Internet of uteruses swollen from PID or penises discharging pus from chlamydia is simple enough to do. Look for visuals of people wasting away from HIV/AIDS. *Show them what this looks like.*

> This is important. Whether parents realize it or not, we have a real problem today. We have fourteen-year-old girls having hysterectomies because of high-risk HPV-causing cervical cancer.
>
> —Diane J. Brown

See, it's easy for your teen to say, "I'm going to be abstinent" when they're sitting across the table from you with a glass of cola in one hand and a look of surety in their eyes. But when that soft drink changes to an alcoholic beverage, and they're locked in passion's embrace with their sweetheart, the story changes. Don't come down too hard on them, though. Any of us could have a moment of weakness.

While media shows various levels of intimacy, it rarely if ever shows the aforementioned diseased body parts. Media may even attempt a few movies-of-the-week, showing a young girl or guy suddenly being faced with teen parenthood. However, you and I both know that ten seconds of a baby crying on film and a cut to the teen mom or dad hoisting herself or himself out of bed and dragging over to the make-shift crib doesn't put a dent in the reality of an infant crying all night … every night. Of feedings every two hours. Of dirty diapers that have to be changed … *all the time.* Of hours sitting in a pediatrician's office with other screaming tots, waiting to see the doctor. Of having to pack up the entire house, it seems, just to go to the grocery store. Of trying to figure out what necessity you can give up to afford a simple jar of Gerber baby food.

But that's the reality, isn't it? Be creative and bold when it comes to showing your teens the consequences of sex outside of marriage. Remind them, too, that you are in it with them. The rules don't change just because you're married. Their being able to honor God and themselves by remaining pure in their teen years will enable them to honor God and their spouses in their adult years as well.

> Growing up, the fear of disappointing my parents was always pretty strong on my mind. Sometimes the thought of admitting to having sex was scarier than the thought of telling them I was pregnant or had an STD. Sometimes just that thought alone kept me from doing anything I knew I'd regret later.
>
> —Jessica Everson

ABSTINENCE PROGRAMS

Do abstinence programs work? According to Diane J. Brown, project director of ThinkSmart Abstinence Education Program out of

Orlando, Florida, they do. "We've seen a 24 percent decrease in teen pregnancy since we started this program six years ago," she said.

In the Florida-based program, students are taught more than just sex education. They are taught critical thinking skills, goal setting, and self-esteem. One of the most important components of the project is helping them to understand *who they are*. By knowing who they are, they are not so easily swayed by popular culture, media giants, and peers.[4]

The December 9, 2002, *Newsweek* cover displayed an attractive teen girl leaning on the shoulders of an equally attractive teen boy. He has her legs locked around his waist as they smile demurely for the camera. "The New Virginity" the headline reads. "Why More Teens Are Choosing Not to Have Sex," followed by the subtitle "The Politics of Abstinence."

Politics? You bet. On page 67 the caption reads: "The Bush (George W.) administration wants to spend millions more selling teens on the virtues of virginity. Not everyone thinks that's such a good idea."

While Bush pushes, church, social, and educational organizations scramble for grant money to fund their own programs. They believe—as do we—that by spending money to teach our teens the truth about themselves and about sex, we will—in the end—save money by controlling disease and out-of-wedlock pregnancies, both of which often lead to government-funded medical care and assistance for the life of the child. More important, we will save lives.

While some authorities say the programs aren't working, others say otherwise. For sure it depends on the quality of the program. (While some programs encourage total abstinence, others teach things like how to use a condom properly.) If your teen is involved in such a program, get involved too. If there isn't such a program in your area, remember that education begins at home. Then, if you feel God so moving you, find out what you need to do to start a program in your area.

PLEDGES AND CONTRACTS

> Parents matter. Teens say parents influence their sexual-decision making more than any other source.
>
> —TeenPregnancy.org

Part of the plan of many abstinence programs is the signing of purity contracts between officials/teachers/program directors and teens. You do not have to have a state-funded or church-funded program to do this, however. You can make your own purity contract between your child and you. "Those are *the most* affective," Diane J. Brown told me in a recent phone conversation.

SECOND VIRGINITY

Perhaps when you sit down to have this talk with your son or daughter you discover that they've already had sex. That they regret it, but it happened. What do you do?

First, *touch them.* Place a gentle hand on their hand, their arm, their shoulder. This lets them know you still love them. Tell them you are sorry this happened, but even more sorry they felt they had to carry the guilt alone. Then, pray with them, asking the Lord to cover that sin. Even if they've already done this, it will be good if you pray with them. Finally, talk about "second virginity."

Second virginity holds to the truth Paul wrote in 2 Corinthians 5:17: "Therefore, if anyone is in Christ, he is a new creation; the old has gone, the new has come!" Remind your son or daughter that sexual sin is just like any other sin; it must submit to the forgiving power of the blood of Jesus. Second virginity also allows them to enter their marriage bed pure with the one they will spend the rest of their lives with.

With all the hope of the previous two chapters, keep in mind—and remind your teen—that once he or she has experienced sex, it is more difficult to say no the next time. They may begin to rationalize, "Why bother to say no?" Talk about this in advance, rather than just hoping they figure it out as they experience it.

IT'S SIMPLY OKAY TO SAY NO

Part of your role as a parent is to help your teen find personal reasons for saying no and to help them develop a plan for saying no. Help them determine ahead of time what they will do in certain situations. Think about this carefully before you begin talking. Don't sit down and say, "Okay ... um ... let's say ... um ... you're at a party and um...."

Your teen will quickly turn you off. Think back to your old days of dating and temptation. Maybe even talk about some of the things that happened to you, so they know you are fully aware of where they are during this time of their lives.

Talk about their plans for the future and write down these goals and what it will take to accomplish them. Then make a list of what will squash those plans and dreams.

Armed with a plan, your teens will then be able to simply say no. And feel *really* good about it.

JESSICA'S BLOG

Parents, allow me to be forthright and speak from the standpoint of an unmarried young woman. You must tell your sons and daughters that if you're going to remain abstinent:

■ You must always be in control of the situation/environment you find yourself in. For boys, you know this will be especially difficult. You will receive more pressure from your peers than females. When your friends call

you to come hang out with some "hot chicks," it will be
challenging to protect yourself when you know they may
find it "uncool." Which leads into my next point ...

■ Find friends and especially a boyfriend or girlfriend
who think like you on the issues of sex and abstinence.

■ Remember that more people are willing to do wrong
or take the easy way out. So choosing to do the right
thing means doing things differently than most everyone around you. Of course, going against the crowd
will be difficult at times. But regardless of how it
appears, it's just as hard for those who take the easy
way out. And they won't ever reach the heights you
will!

■ Make a list (on paper) of reasons not to have sex and
why you choose abstinence for yourself. Make a new
list every month and sign it. Read it one quick time
daily. Doing this will make it part of your subcon-
scious. Then everything you do on a day-to-day basis
will subconsciously be to benefit those things.

■ Be positive about your decision concerning sex and
abstinence. For instance, if while getting prepared for a
date you are debating with yourself just how far you
will allow things to go, more often than not an "I
don't know" at the beginning will lead to a "much
more than I planned" by the end.

■ Realize that "but we really love each other" isn't a reason to have sex but a reason not to. If you care about a
relationship, you will protect it from all the pitfalls of
a sexual relationship. Don't make your relationship
vulnerable by leaving the grace of God.

■ Who cares if you lose someone because you won't have
sex or perform some other type of sexual act? Did you
really lose anything worth keeping? Some years back I
started dating a guy I really thought a lot of ... at first.
I met him through a group of friends, and sometimes

we would double date with other couples and singles in the group. One night, after a couple of months of knowing him, the whole group decided to go out together. He called me while I was getting ready to tell me he was bringing a girl who (as he put it) "thought more of him because she would have sex with him." Well, I still went out with my friends that night and—long story short—he made a fool of himself, and I learned a valuable lesson. I'm just glad I found out so quickly what type of guy he was. Imagine if I had slept with him; it would have taken longer to find out who he really was, and I would have lost so much more. You never want someone like that to get the best of you. So don't give it to them!

- Don't take all your advice from someone who isn't a virgin. I've never understood that; how can someone who isn't a virgin tell you about being one? How can someone who doesn't have a blessed sexual relationship tell you about one?

- Guys, take a good look through your spiritual eyes at the way a lot of guys are living these days. Why is it that as a whole, guys don't realize the way they are degrading themselves? We focus so much on girls valuing themselves enough to stay pure, why don't we do the same for guys? A friend of mine once referred to himself as different because unlike most of his friends, he valued his body and his spirit enough that he wasn't willing to have sex with anything that moved. If you will be the future "head of the household" and (as the Bible says) "loving your wife as Christ loved the church, willing to die for her," shouldn't you begin practicing that kind of love now?

- Keep a strong faith in God that he will bless you for your decision. You have to believe that ultimately he is in control and that if you trust him and do what he tells you, then there are more blessings on their way to you. Then you need to use your time productively because "faith without works is dead." Work to become the person he created you to be.

Jessica's Q & A Blog

An interview with teens choosing abstinence:

Now you tell me: What made you decide on abstinence?

Missy (sixteen, Idaho): I decided on abstinence because, for one, it's just the right thing to do, but second, I think of an analogy that I was taught a long time ago. At birth you are given purity, which can be symbolized by a piece of duct tape, and the more you use your duct tape and stick it on other guys the duller it becomes. Then once you find the one you are supposed to be with for the rest of your life (your husband), your duct tape is so used it's lost all its stick; therefore, your marriage isn't held together as well as it would have been if you had saved your duct tape just for your husband. I want to keep my duct tape sticky!

DJ (seventeen, Tennessee): My faith was my main reason for deciding to remain a virgin. The hard part is, you hear from all of your youth leaders and such "don't have sex because of this or this," but really you have to make the decision for yourself. My number one reason is because God tells us not to, but I have others because I am human and sometimes just want not to listen to God and enjoy life. I believe God blesses those who wait for marriage. I believe it will make my marriage more enjoyable on that end because I won't have other things to compare it to or guilt to deal with. Health reasons are last on my list, but they are there.

How difficult is it today to be a teen and stay pure?

Missy: Peer pressure is a major struggle as a teen these days. The number of things to be pressured about keeps rising as society standards keep dropping. Nobody cares anymore about becoming a high achiever and/or setting high goals for themselves so they can feel accomplished in something. All it is anymore is being able to go out and have a good time. Nobody has good moral values in their life ... and the fact that most parents don't care what their children are up to, and sometimes even support them in what they are doing, doesn't really help the situation either! Sorry, I kinda got off on a trail ... but straight to the point ... yes, it is bad for those of us who don't do it already and don't plan to do it at all!

DJ: Very difficult. I don't care how strong any person thinks they are, Christian or not. It is difficult. My girlfriend and I have to constantly keep in check, because we both know that if one or both of us do not have our guard up, we may make a mistake. Now that doesn't mean you have to walk around living in fear of touching each other or something stupid like that.

Set up strict boundaries and have people around you who can make sure you are following those boundaries. Even with that, it is still hard because the choice is always there. I can't make the right choice on my own, so I daily rely on God to help me stay pure, because I believe that purity is the highest form of worship to God, and I want to live a life of worship.

What helps you the most in keeping your commitment?

Missy: I believe being a strong Christian really helps and makes it much easier to deal with it all. When you are a strong Christian, you will always know that you have God there to help you through it, and he will never leave your side. Even if all of your friends decide you're not cool enough because you don't do the stuff they do. God will most definitely always be there ... I mean, he didn't die on the cross for nothing!

DJ: I believe that as Christians one of the best ways we can live a life of worship is by remaining pure. That is a mark of a true follower of Christ in my opinion. Christians may not want to admit it, but if we know a fellow believer who has had sex before marriage, we don't look at them the same way. It is one of those sins that just comes out in the open and shocks other believers. I could go on another hour on how horribly the church handles that situation, but that wasn't the question.

Anyway, so besides wanting to live a life of worship, having people around you who aren't afraid to ask you how things are going is critical. If you don't have people who care, then you won't care. Plain and simple. I know that if my girlfriend and I are in certain places where we know that no one could give a rip if we had sex, the temptation level is much higher. So keep good mentors and friends around you to help, and ask God for strength because we really can't win this fight on our own.

Interview with a teen who is a Christian and has chosen "temporary abstinence":

IS ABSTINENCE A DECISION YOU'VE MADE TO KEEP UNTIL MARRIAGE?

Brian (seventeen, Southern California): No, this is not a commitment that I have made until marriage. I personally don't see it as important as a lot of people do. Marriage isn't something that necessarily lasts forever, so for me to wait until that time seems pretty pointless. I don't think my spouse will love me any more or less if I was or wasn't a virgin when we get married. I only know about one out of maybe twenty people that claim to be virgins. And out of those that claim that, they [all] say that they *aren't* waiting till marriage, they say that they are waiting for the "right one." So it's just a matter of time until that person is no longer a virgin. So, what are the chances of me marrying a virgin? I just don't see it as "sacred" as it's cracked up to be.

Interview with a teen who is Christian but sexually active:

WHAT WOULD YOU SAY TO CHRISTIAN PARENTS ABOUT CHRISTIAN TEEN SEXUALITY?

Rachel (not her real name, sixteen, Georgia): I would say, "Listen. Kids—even good kids who go to church every week and participate in youth group and all that—are having sex. They struggle with it, sure. We do. We know we've done something or are doing something that God doesn't necessarily want us doing, but the fight is just too much at times, you know?

What's really awful is some of the places we're doing it. I mean, yeah, I know they're awful, but even more awful is that parents are clueless. We're doing it at school, at church youth camps, and at parties and stuff. We're even doing it in our own homes.

HOW CAN CHRISTIAN PARENTS HELP THEIR TEENS MAKE ABSTINENCE A CHOICE?

Rachel: Sometimes I think that if teens are gonna do it, they're just gonna do it. For whatever reason, whether it be that we're planning to marry one day, or we're thinking God will forgive us, or we're placing bets on whether or not we'll one day get married, ask God to forgive us, and then go from there. But parents need to quit being so trusting. I mean, for goodness sakes, don't give us so much freedom. You let us stay home alone for hours at a time and our boyfriend or girlfriend comes over, and what do you think is gonna happen?

WHAT I'M WONDERING IS THIS: WHAT ABOUT THE RISKS? OR PREGNANCY? STDS? THE EMOTIONAL RISKS THAT MIGHT AFFECT YOUR LIFE AFTER YOU DO GET MARRIED?

Rachel: Mmmm. I dunno about all that. I mean, pregnancy and STDs, yeah. You'd have to be living on another planet. But about the last part. That's a pretty good point. I'll have to think on that one.

CHAPTER 9

Sex, Lies, and the Rest of Their Lives

Or, For This Reason

For this reason a man will leave his father and mother and be united to his wife, and they shall become one flesh.

—GENESIS 2:24

When I was in high school," a friend told me recently, "I dated a guy for about two years—off and on, but mostly on. We were so 'hot' for each other, but we kept ourselves in check. We never had sex." There was a bit of a twinkle in her eye as she added, "But we wanted to. Oh, gosh, how we wanted to.

"Funny thing is, I still have the diaries I wrote in back then. Nearly every line of every page is filled with my dreams of what I thought life was going to be like once we were able to get married." She giggled. "I used to think we'd fall into each other's arms every night, and we'd spend Saturday nights with our friends and then on Sundays ... oh, Sundays! On Sundays we would get up, go to church, have lunch with my family or his, then go home and make love all day until late in the night and then on Monday we'd get up and go to work like all the other normal people in the world."

I know for a fact that she didn't marry this guy, so I asked her what happened. She shrugged. "One minute we were in love, and the next we weren't. One minute we were in high school, and the next I was graduating from college and engaged to another man."

I asked if she had the same visions of physical rapture while dating her now-husband as she had in high school. "Absolutely!" she exclaimed, then she shook her head. "Not that it mattered. I've been married an awful lot of years now and not one single Sunday did I spend making love all day and into the night. Not one."

When we're in high school, we have some fairly rapturous misconceptions about married life. We grow up and learn that we most definitely had gotten it wrong. For the most part, we thought marriage was all about *finally* getting to have sex. While, in part, that's true, marriage is about so much more than sex.

How can we teach our children the beauty of marriage, especially considering the divorce rate in the country? Even among Christians. What grains of truth can we give them—whether we're married to their fathers or mothers or not—that will help them build the character needed for becoming godly men and women, husbands and wives, mothers and fathers?

LOVE STORY

There are some beautiful stories in the Bible that I challenge you to tell your children, beginning when they are old enough to appreciate a good story, adding various levels of truth that they are mature enough to understand. Begin with Adam and Eve. End with Jesus and His bride.

Listed below are some names and thoughts:

> *Adam and Eve:* When Eve was created, she was pure and was brought to Adam by her Heavenly Father. Later on, when there was temptation, and when that temptation was yielded to, everyone suffered (Gen. 2:4—3:24).

> *Abraham and Sarah:* The story of Abraham and Sarah gives us more than a few points, including the heartbreak of infertility and moving from one place to

another. Within the context of their story, however, is a tale of a loving couple, devoted to each other (Gen. 12—23).

Isaac and Rebekah: The story of these two lovers is so beautiful, mainly because it is a foreshadowing of the Bride of Christ. As you talk to your teens about this story, focus on the elements necessary for Isaac's bride (she had to be willing, she had to be of the blood line,[1] and she was richly gifted when she said yes[2]) (Gen. 24).

> "For this reason a man will leave his father and mother and be united to his wife, and the two will become one flesh." This is a profound mystery—but I am talking about Christ and the church.
>
> —Ephesians 5:31–32
> (quoting Genesis 2:24)

Jacob and Rachel: Jacob was willing to do anything for Rachel, including working for her father for fourteen years. This story can teach teens the importance of familial approval, and is a good story to share with your teen son about his role of protector and provider of the one he loves (Gen. 28:10—29:30).

Boaz and Ruth: When Boaz saw Ruth gleaning in his fields, he was immediately concerned about her physical safety. Again, this is a good story for your son, teaching him his role of protecting the virtue and physical self of a woman who may be his or another man's wife some day. For your daughter, this story will help her see the power of submitting to her husband. Though Ruth didn't understand everything Boaz told her to do, she rested in the knowledge that every choice he made on her behalf was one of godly wisdom, prayerfully attained. (See the entire book of Ruth.)

Solomon and the Shulamite: Passion. Yes! There is passion in marriage, and it is of God. We were made to delight in each other's physical bodies *in marriage.* (See the entire book of the Song of Solomon.)

Jesus and His bride: Share the Scriptures found in Genesis 2:24 and Ephesians 5:31–32. (There is actually a detailed teaching here, but this is not the book for it.)

THE COUPLE IN THE MIRROR

If you are married, and in a good marriage, your life can be the greatest example of God's intent for marriage that your children will ever see. If your marriage is not good, then perhaps you can point your teen to family or friends whose marriages have a solid foundation and who enjoy good relationships.

If you are not married—if you are a single parent—you still have an opportunity to show your children the value of a good marriage by allowing them to observe your relationship with God. The relationship we have in marriage is the closest thing we have to our heavenly marriage with Jesus.

MARRIAGE PREPARATION

I was stunned. A young man who'd recently slipped a ring on the third finger of his sweetheart's left hand bemoaned the fact that she wanted to go to premarital classes before setting the date for their wedding. He was vehemently against it. I was stunned.

I asked him what he did for a living. He told me where he worked, what his position was, that he worked about fifty hours a week, and that he already had retirement in his sights for twenty years from when he first began working.

I asked him how long he went to school to learn to do what he does for about fifty hours per week.

He answered, "Four years."

"Four years," I said. "For something you do fifty hours a week and plan to do for only twenty years."

"That's right," he said with a nod.

I asked him how long the marriage classes were.

"An hour a week for six weeks."

"So, six hours," I said.

"Right."

"How many hours a week do you think you'll be married?"

He gave me a quizzical look. "I'll be married all week."

"Sooooo …" I calculated mentally, "One hundred and sixty eight hours per week."

I watched him do the math. "Right."

"And how many years will you be married?" I asked.

He furrowed his brow. "I don't know. I mean, I'm planning for the rest of my life. I'm twenty-six now, so … we could make it more than fifty years. Maybe sixty."

"All right then. You gave four years to a career you spend fifty hours a week times twenty years at, but you won't give six hours to the most important relationship of your life, which—according to you— will be for one hundred and sixty-eight hours times fifty-two weeks times fifty or sixty years. Does that really make sense?"

The young man called his sweetheart and agreed to attend pre-marital classes.

A Major in Marriage with a Minor in Children

Marriage is one of the most wonderful unions you can ever experience. It's also full of rocky roads and dry valleys.

I am writing these words while sitting in the front passenger seat of my car, typing away on my laptop. My husband of nearly thirty years is sitting next to me, driving toward our Central Florida home. We're on our way back from Georgia where our daughter, son-in-law, and new granddaughter live. We have just taken a couple of days off from our busy schedules to see that precious "little peanut" for the first time since her birth a few weeks ago.

I feel all warm and gooey inside. My husband and I have laughed and giggled with each other over the past few hours. We are content.

But it wasn't always that way. That same daughter was a strong-willed child. Many times she exasperated us. Many times we argued over the problems we had in raising her. But that same child has grown up to be a fine woman of God. She's a good mother and a fine wife. She makes us proud, and we're content.

My husband and I are not wealthy, but financially we can breathe. There were times—when there were lots of mouths to feed, and feet to put shoes on, and backs to put clothes on, and teeth to put braces on, and eyes to put glasses on, and extracurricular activities to pay for—when we basically robbed Peter to pay Paul to survive. Finances (or lack thereof) can put a real strain on a marriage.

There were times when I was sick and times when my husband was sick. Illness can also put a real strain on a marriage.

When marriage is under the effects of the various strains, when the vows are tested beyond measure, guess what suffers along with it? The marriage bed. And, yes, our marriage bed has suffered from time to time over the years.

But right now we are content. Our marriage is strong. We're grounded spiritually as we've never been before. Life is pretty sweet. Marriage feels like everything it's supposed to be.

Our children (not just mine; I'm talking to all of us now) need to know that marriage won't be all about sex. It will be filled with joy and sorrow, good days and bad, vacations and work days. *It's the toughest job you'll ever love.*

Well ... that and parenthood.

JESSICA'S Q & A BLOG

NOW YOU TELL ME: WHAT METHODS DID YOU USE TO HELP YOUR CHILD STAY PURE BEFORE MARRIAGE?

Kathleen (wife, parent, publisher): Our daughter's purity was of utmost importance to her father and me. We had a set of rules that we meant for her to observe, no matter what we had to do to ensure it. We didn't just come up with a set of rules, her behavior warranted the rules.

First, no riding alone in cars with boys. We felt she did not have the maturity to ride alone with a boy yet. When she was able to show us she could make good sound decisions, we agreed the rule would be lifted. We embraced all of her friends hanging out at our house so we could get to know them.

Second, we kept her so busy with sports and church activities, she was too tired to do much of anything else. That was important. Keeping her busy. When asked at her bridal shower what were her favorite memories of her school years, she said without a doubt that basketball and youth group were the time of her life. We made sure to keep balance and not overwhelm her with activities, so homework was taken care of and family time was possible.

Third, anything she said, we checked up on. We knew she was capable of lying to us. She was going to a friend's house? Good. Give me the phone number, and let me call her parent. If she got upset about that, there was a reason for it. She knew I was capable of checking up on her at any time. This was my job as her mother, and I took it seriously. You have to take it seriously.

She also couldn't date, except in a group, until we felt she had the maturity to do so. It was a big decision to let our daughter go off in a car with a young man we didn't know or trust, and they both needed to prove to us that they understood what our rules were and why they were in place. The timing was all up to them. They had the ability to prove it to us at any time. In her junior year, she met the young man who would one day be her husband. My husband and I told them that if they wanted to date, they needed a third person or another couple. They hated that, but years later at their wedding, it was brought up during the best man's toast. Years later, they thanked us.

I remember the first time he came to get her in his car. This was a big moment. My husband took him aside and said, "I'm a hunter. I have a gun. I will use it. If you stop this car with my daughter in it for anything longer than a stop sign or a red light, I will find out about it. I will hunt you down, and I will shoot you." Of course, he knew my husband wouldn't literally shoot him, but he also knew my husband meant what he said about our daughter's purity being of utmost importance to us. My husband told him, "Her purity may not be important to you, but it is everything to me."

We made this of utmost importance in the raising of our daughter.

Today, she and her husband are in ministry. My daughter and her husband now have a little girl of their own. Now they really understand.

CHAPTER 10

Hope and Help for Parents of Today's High School Students

Waiting for the arrival of puberty to discuss their [sexuality] with your child is like chasing a train which has already left the station.

—DR. PAUL C. REISSOR,
PARENTS' GUIDE TO TEEN HEALTH

Think you'll never get through these four years? You will, we promise. Whether in one piece or tattered and torn, however, is another thing.

Good news! There is hope and help! Before we look at the list of Web sites you can visit or books you can read, let's go over a few little tips.

- Above all, pray! Pray continually, the apostle Paul said (1 Thess. 5:17). Paul was never the father of a modern teen, but he sure helped bring to spiritual maturity a generation of believers.
- While you're praying, find areas in your teen's life to praise. The words "I am so proud of you" mean so much to a child who no longer seems to know his or her own mind or body.
- Be quick to apologize when you are wrong. It's okay to be wrong. Maybe you made a hasty assumption, and now you have to go to your teen and eat a little crow. You'll teach your child so much more in your apology than you ever could in your refusal to do so.
- While we're on that subject ... try not to overreact about every little thing. "Pick your battles," my

husband used to say. (I should have listened better. I was typically the parent who went off half-cocked. Honestly, it's a miracle my children and I survived at all.) The best way to keep yourself from having your "hot buttons" pushed is to know them. For example, when I'm on the road, traveling as a speaker or on a book tour, I try not to have any communication with those who have a propensity to make me say or do something I regret later. My husband says if I'm coming home late on Sunday, I should tell everyone that I won't be available until after Monday and then spend Monday on the sofa with neither home nor cell phone service available. And he's right. I tried it and it works!

- And while we are on *that* subject: Nurture your-selves as parents. Nurture yourselves an individuals. Nurture yourselves as a married couple (if you are). Nurture friendships and hobbies, and especially nurture your relationship with God.

- Speaking of hobbies, find common interests with your high school teen and then *do them*. Plan getaways—whether to dinner, to a ball game, to the mall (the one place Jessica and I found common ground!), or even away for a weekend at the beach or mountains or fishing or whatever. Just make sure you *both* enjoy it.

- Find common meeting grounds. My friend Janice tells a story about the time her father—a great lover of music—asked her to allow him to listen to one whole album of her choice and then she would listen to one whole album of his choice. It was the '60s, and while Janice also loved music (as a teen she was already a classical pianist), she dearly loved to push a few boundaries with her dad. So she came to the meeting ground with a Rolling Stones album in her hand. For the next hour or so, she and her father listened to Mick and friends belt out the music. Strangely, her father found things about it he liked ... and some things about it that he didn't. Then it was his turn. He brought out his album, Dvorak's *New World Symphony*, written in the late 1800s. At first—and quite naturally—Janice assumed she'd simply have to suffer through. Instead, she fell in love with the music, absconded with the album, and it remains among her favorite music to this day. Her father, however, still isn't crazy about the Rolling Stones.

> Every generation needs men of courage, men of conviction, men of strength—men of God.
>
> —Joshua Harris,
> *Not Even a Hint*

- Don't give your teen an easy path to sexual activity and promiscuity. While you may think this is a no-brainer, you'd be surprised. As a society we make it too easy for our children to respond to each other sexually. We inundate them with sexual messages, give them enormous amounts of free time and/or money, and allow them to participate in unsupervised activities. The old saying is "If you don't want to fight the bull, stay out of the pen." These words have been used to encourage teens to stay away from sexual temptation, but they can also be useful for parents. In other words, be proactive in the war against teens and sex. Talk to them, talk to them, talk to them. (And then be ready to listen.)

TALK TO THEM, TALK TO THEM, TALK TO THEM

Here's something you won't find shocking: parents aren't spending enough time with their teens. I have concluded that time is one of the greatest gifts you can give to them. Forget the toys, the cars, CD player, and Xbox. Give them T.I.M.E.

> **T: Touch.** Touch your children. Even in their nearly grown bodies, they are still the little tots we used to rock to sleep and the infants we cradled as they took their feedings. There is seldom a time when a human doesn't respond positively to a loving touch. Touch your children.
>
> **I: Inspire them.** Inspire them by encouraging their talents and by praising their hard work. Inspire them to do great things. Inspire them with your own life. Above all, inspire them to grow in Christ daily.
>
> **M: Meals and Wheels.** Eat your meals as a family around a table. When you do, talk about their day. You may want to play the "best thing that happened today/worst thing that happened today" game. When you are in the car together, turn the tunes down low (or off!) and talk to them. Encourage them to share with you by asking them questions—not general questions but real questions—about their daily lives.
>
> **E: Entertainment.** In spite of media's negative influence, you can find plenty of teachable moments within it. You can also *do things* together. Both you and your teen like good movies? Go! (Or rent!) Both you and your teen like music? Attend a concert together. You both like art? Get tickets to a museum and make a day of it. If you both like sports, participate together.

T.I.M.E. is "time consuming." But I promise you will not regret any second, minute, or hour you spend with your teen.

THE WISDOM OF A PARENT

When I was a teenager and in the dating game, my father handed me a dime and told me to keep it on my person at all times. "If a boy ever gets fresh … if he ever asks if he can do something sexual with you … hand him this dime."

"Okaaaaay," I said. Knowing that a condom was that same price, I thought my father had lost his mind.

My father continued. "Then you tell him, 'Here's a dime. You go call my father. If it's okay with him, it's okay with me.'"

Ah. The wisdom of a parent.

Your children should be learning about sex—every bit of it, the good, the bad, and the ugly of it—from *you.* Sure, they'll take classes in school. Yes, they'll hear things on the playground at school or in the locker room before and after PE. They could even find pornographic materials in any variety of places, which will only distort the truth about sex.

But they need to hear the majority of it from *you.*

Not all at once, of course, but over the course of their young lives. And not as though you're telling them some dark secret. *This is God's gift to the bride and groom!* (Remember the story of Adam and Eve?) But as you tell them the beauty of married sex, you must be a brave enough … wise enough … parent to tell them the stuff you'd just as soon they'd never have to hear. Because the truth is, they *will* hear it.

A FINAL WORD FROM EVA MARIE

Over the past few years I have learned a couple of important things. (Actually, I've learned more than two, but these are two that are pertinent to the end of this book.)

One: I can talk to God while I'm taking a shower.

For a long time when I was raising kids, holding down two jobs, and trying to keep my head above water, it felt like this was the only time I really had to talk to him at all. At first it was kind of embarrassing. As a child I always got dressed up to go to church. As an adult I get dressed to go to church (though not necessarily in a dress since I'm a Floridian). So talking to God in my birthday suit was a bit difficult, even though I knew he knows what I look like without my clothes on.

Then I thought about Eve, who walked with God in the cool of the evening without a stitch on before he became the first couturier and made her that animal-fur ensemble. Then I thought about the time the three angels came to see Abraham and Sarah. The Bible tells us one of those angels was "the Lord." He told Abraham that he would return in a year and that Sarah would have had a child by that time.

Sarah overheard the conversation and "laughed in her heart." The Lord turned to her and said, "Why did you laugh?" Embarrassed, Sarah said, "I did not laugh." Then the Lord turned back to Abraham and gave the promise of his son, Isaac. Looking back over his shoulder, the Lord said to Sarah, "You did too laugh."

Thousands of years later, when Jesus walked the earth as a man, He spoke to a paralytic, saying that his "sins were forgiven." The teachers of the Law said *to themselves,* "This man is blaspheming."

The Scriptures tell us in Matthew 9:4–6: "Knowing their thoughts, Jesus said, 'Why do you entertain evil thoughts in your hearts? Which is easier: to say, 'Your sins are forgiven,' or to say, 'Get up and walk'? But so that you may know that the Son of Man has authority on earth to forgive sins....' Then he said to the paralytic, 'Get up, take your mat and go home.'"

It's really cool when we know God knows what we think; if that's the case, we can afford to stand naked before him, both spiritually and physically. We can pray in the shower and not be ashamed. We can also be assured that Jesus knows our every thought. Sometimes—as in the case of the teachers—it can be *scary.* More often, comforting.

Second, I have learned that if we can stand before God unashamed and tell him all the things on our minds, then we can unashamedly tell our teens the truth about God's love for them, his plan for their lives, his desire for their purity, and Satan's plan to sabotage all of that.

Tell them the truth.

Tell them *the truth*.

JESSICA'S BLOG

Parents, you must understand that your teens' world is different from yours, but—at the same time—there are still a lot of similarities. Mom and Dad, share stories on all subjects with your child about things you have learned and would have done differently. Make yourself approachable. Have time for them. Don't avoid certain subjects because they make you uncomfortable. You must open the lines of communication, or they will forever remain closed.

Dad, here's a special word for you: Your role should not be just a disciplinary one, and your relationship should not be, let's say, just about sports. When you spend time with your son or daughter, you can't always be just passing time. Regardless of what's going on in your life, make your child feel like you enjoy being around him or her.

Your kids won't even think about sex as leaving God's grace if they already feel apart from him. Make sure you are there to guide your children of all ages in their relationships with God.

Don't be afraid to have different rules for different kids. All teens are different and have different weaknesses and needs.

Sit down and talk with your kids about each new freedom they receive as they mature. Teach them freedoms come with responsibilities by making sure each new freedom you give them comes with a new responsibility. Stick to it. If they don't keep up with one particular responsibility, take away the freedom you have tied to it. They will grow more disciplined, and that's what they're going to need to live righteously.

Teach your kids that the battle for their souls is a daily one and not a one-time-only thing.

Don't try to be friends with your kids. I heard it put best while I was watching one of the popular plays from the Tyler Perry (who wrote *Diary of a Mad Black Woman*) collection. Medea, one of the main characters in his plays, said to her daughter (concerning her granddaughter) "That's the problem … you're trying to be your child's friend. Let them tell you what they're gonna do. How are you gonna be your child's friend? When they help you pay a light bill or a phone bill or the rent, then you can be friends."[1]

Very funny and very true. There will come a time when your relationship can be more like friends, but it's not when they're being raised in your home.

Kids are bored. Get your kids active in something that will give them a sense of purpose.

Remember life lessons don't come in one afternoon's discussion. They come with consistency and a little each day along the way.

It is hard out there for kids to remain pure. You can take some of the fight off of their shoulders by simply not setting them too free. This is for boys, too, because it seems even in Christian homes, boys are often given more freedom than their sisters. Your kids may not appreciate your restrictions, but that's because they won't realize until later how much easier you have made it for them. That said, kids do still need some room to grow, experiment, experience, make mistakes, and learn on their own. Better they do it now when they're in your home than when you aren't there to help them.

Don't make the mistake of thinking you or your restrictions will protect them. They are still going to be in battle over this every day, and the best thing you can do for them is arm them for the fight by arming them with God's Word.

Readers' Guide

For Personal Reflection and Group Study

Helping young people make it through high school in one piece requires a lot of thought, prayer, and important conversations. This book was designed to equip you as a parent to help your teenager make wise choices and to help make the teenage years as smooth as possible. It is never easy to raise a teenager, but with open communication and preparation for the issues that come along, the high school years don't have to be too rocky. Hopefully, by reading this book, you've already begun to formulate positive strategies for dealing with the realities of high school alongside your son or daughter.

This study guide should help you continue to formulate these strategies. The questions that follow are designed to help you further process what you have read. They should also help you personalize the advice in this book by applying it to your own situation. Additionally, each set of questions is accompanied by Scripture passages to encourage you and keep your perspective on the Lord. After all, there is no better perspective to have, no matter the situation!

Use these questions and Scripture passages in discussion groups to come up with effective tactics for coping with the problems that may accompany your teenager's high school experience. Use them to come up with conversation starters to help you engage your teenager in important discussions. Use them to help you prepare a game plan to help your teenager face the problems and temptations they will certainly meet along the way.

Above all, remember that the Lord has a plan for everyone's life, even the life of your high school student. No matter what, he is still in control!

Chapter 1
Sex, Lies, and the Teen Years

Scripture references: Ephesians 6:1–4; Proverbs 15:1–5

1. Can you describe a time recently when you felt like your teenager changed overnight or in which you wondered what happened to your "baby"?

2. How can you show your child that you are comfortable with discussing his or her sexuality and thus encourage healthy conversations about it?

3. How has your teenager recently begun to explore his or her identity by challenging some of your beliefs?

4. What are at least two aspects of your teen's life in which you can become actively interested?

5. How can you use this interest to create learning opportunities?

CHAPTER 2
SEX, LIES, AND HEARTTHROBS

Scripture references: Exodus 20:1–6; 1 John 2:15–17

1. Who were some of your personal "idols" as a teenager, and how did you express your admiration for them?

2. How does your experience compare and contrast with your teenager's personal "idols" today?

3. Why is it so important to keep track of the famous people your teenager admires?

4. What are some teachable moments you can think of in the lives of celebrities that you might be able to share with your teen?

5. In what ways can you try to become one of the more influential role models in your teenager's life?

CHAPTER 3
SEX, LIES, AND FASHION

Scripture references: 1 Peter 3:3–4; Colossians 3:12–14

1. Along with Abercrombie & Fitch, what other brand names or celebrities in today's society promote sexual messages to teenagers?

2. Why is it so important for parents to keep up-to-date on these messages and the various advertising campaigns that teenagers face?

3. How can you make your teenager aware of the importance of sexual integrity, both for males and females, even beyond abstinence?

4. In what ways does modesty, or lack of modesty, relate to personal self-worth?

5. How can you encourage your teenager to express his or her personal style while also encouraging the value of modesty?

CHAPTER 4
SEX, LIES, AND SPRING BREAK

Scripture references: 2 Samuel 11:1–5; Proverbs 23:19–22

1. What aspects of the history of spring break do you find interesting, especially in relationship to the spring break of today's society?

2. Which of the various spring-break practices listed in this chapter disturb you the most?

3. Which of the various positive alternatives to these practices do you think your teenager would enjoy most?

4. Why do you think the concept of a "break" from everyday life is so appealing to humans, even to the point of causing us to relax our standards and morals for living wholesomely?

5. How can you as a parent help make spring break fun for your teenager while also setting boundaries that protect him or her from making bad choices?

CHAPTER 5
SEX, LIES, AND THE PROM

Scripture references: 1 Corinthians 10:31–33; Matthew 6:28–33

1. Before you read this chapter, what has been your typical impression of the prom and all that it should involve?

2. How has this impression changed after reading this chapter?

3. Why is a conversation with your teenager about prom so important, and what issues should you discuss in this conversation?

4. What are some memories that you hope your teenager takes away from the prom?

5. What specific things can you do to help these memories become realities for your teenager?

Chapter 6
Sex, Lies, and Dating 101

Scripture references: Ephesians 6:10–18; 1 Corinthians 15:33

1. What boundaries do you currently have set up for your teenager as far as dating is concerned?

2. What healthy alternatives to the typical "dinner and a movie" date, whether listed in this chapter or from your own experience, do you think your teenager would most enjoy and why?

3. How can you encourage your teenager to cultivate a strong personal identity and sense of self, regardless of whether or not dating is involved?

4. Why is it so important to set up consequences—and follow through with those consequences—if your son or daughter breaks the rules for dating you have created?

5. Why is sexual assault such an important issue to discuss with your teenager, and how can you make sure that you have this discussion?

CHAPTER 7
SEX, LIES, STDS, AND PREGNANCY

Scripture references: 1 Corinthians 6:18–20; Proverbs 5

1. Which of the statistics in this chapter about sexually transmitted diseases struck you the most and why?

2. What do you consider to be some of the "hard questions" for you to personally ask your teen when discussing sex?

3. Why are these questions so difficult to ask and also to discuss?

4. How can the church as a whole come together to love teens who face pregnancy or STDs and help them to make it through?

5. If you found out your son or daughter had an STD or was going to have a baby, what specific things could you do to support your child and show him or her the love of Christ?

CHAPTER 8
SEX, LIES, AND ABSTINENCE

Scripture references: 1 Corinthians 13:4–7, James 1:27

1. What is your personal definition of abstinence?

2. Why do you think the definitions of abstinence and sexual intercourse are so hazy in today's society?

3. How can you encourage your teenager to cultivate friendships with members of the opposite sex and stress emotional intimacy rather than physically intimate relationships?

4. What do you think is the best strategy for dealing with a teenager who has already had sex?

5. What specific creative strategies can you use to make your teenager aware of the consequences that are associated with pre-marital sex and the ways in which they can avoid premarital sex?

CHAPTER 9
SEX, LIES, AND THE REST OF THEIR LIVES

Scripture references: 1 Corinthians 7:1–4; Hebrews 13:4–5

1. What are some of the misconceptions you had as a high school student about marriage, or even about adult life in general?

2. How can you use what you know now to help your teenager create realistic expectations for the future?

3. Which of the love stories found in the Bible do you think your son or daughter could gain the most from and why?

4. What do you think God's idea of a good, healthy marriage would include?

5. In what ways can you help your son or daughter understand and value this type of Christian, healthy marriage?

CHAPTER 10
HOPE AND HELP FOR PARENTS OF TODAY'S HIGH SCHOOL STUDENTS

Scripture references: Deuteronomy 11:18–21; James 1:2–5

1. Currently, what are the biggest challenges you are facing in raising a teenager?

2. What are the biggest joys you have found in raising a teenager?

3. How can you better focus on these joys while working through the challenges and keeping the lines of communication with your teenager open?

4. What are some specific things you can pray for your teenager as you go through these years together?

5. Overall, how can you create quality time together with your teenager so that these years are full of growth in Christ and open communication?

A Few Sources for Help

BOOKS

Anderson, Neil T. *Finding Freedom in a Sex-Obsessed World.* Eugene, OR: Harvest House, 2004.

Austin, Sandy J. *Angry Teens and the Parents Who Love Them.* Kansas City: Beacon Hill Press, 2002.

Clarkson, Sally. *The Ministry of Motherhood.* Colorado Springs: WaterBrook Press, 2004.

———. *The Mission of Motherhood.* Colorado Springs: WaterBrook Press, 2003.

Everson, Eva Marie, and Jessica Everson. *Sex, Lies, and the Media.* Colorado Springs: Cook Communications, 2005.

Gresh, Bob. *Who Moved the Goalpost?* Chicago: Moody Publishers, 2001.

Gresh, Dannah. *And the Bride Wore White.* Chicago: Moody Publishers, 1999.

———. *Secret Keeper.* Chicago: Moody Publishers, 2002.

Ingram, Chip, and Tim Walker. *Sex 180.* Grand Rapids: Baker Books, 2005.

Luce, Ron. *Battle Cry for a Generation.* Colorado Springs: Cook Communications, 2005.

Owens, Terry. *Extreme Marriage.* Colorado Springs: WaterBrook Press, 2005.

Refuel, The Complete New Testament. Nashville: Thomas Nelson, 2004.

Revolve, The Complete New Testament. Nashville: Thomas Nelson, 2003, 2005.

Savage, Jill, and Pam Farrel. *Got Teens?* Eugene, OR: Harvest House, 2005.

Scherrer, David L., and Linda M. Klepacki. *How to Talk to Your Kids About Sexuality.* Colorado Springs: Cook Communications, 2004.

WEB SITES

www.ama-assn.org

www.jama.com

www.youthfire.com/media/compare

www.Christianteens.net

www.ChristianityToday.com/teens

http://www.cwfa.org/main.asp

www.FamilyLife.org

http://www.family.org/

http://friendsfirst.org/

http://www.focusas.com/index.html

www.focusonyourchild.com

www.heartofvirtue.com

www.integritymusic.com

http://www.ncweb.com/org/rapecrisis/sesamehome.html

www.parable.com

www.parenthood.com

www.teenpregnancy.org

Notes

Introduction

1. Carolyn Ruch, e-mail message to author Eva Marie Everson, April 22, 2005.

Chapter 1
Sex, Lies, and the Teen Years

1. Ralph I. Lopez, *The Teen Health Book: A Parents' Guide to Adolescent Health and Well-Being* (New York: W. W. Norton & Co, Inc., 2002), 15.
2. "What is Puberty?" Cool Nurse, http://www.coolnurse.com/puberty.htm.
3. "Sleep Deprivation," Sleepdex, http://www.sleepdex.org/deficit.htm.
4. "What is Puberty?" Cool Nurse, http://www.coolnurse.com/puberty.htm.
5. Drew Pinsky, *Teen Species: Boys,* The Science Channel (BBC/TLC Coproduction), 2002.
6. Lopez, *Teen Health Book,* 47.
7. "What is Puberty?" Cool Nurse, http://www.coolnurse.com/breast_answers.htm.
8. "Sexuality, Contraception and the Media," *Pediatrics 107,* No 1, (2001), American Academy of Pediatrics Committee on Public Education http://www.aap.org/policy/re0038.html.
9. Lopez, *Teen Health Book,* 177.

CHAPTER 2
SEX, LIES, AND HEARTTHROBS

1. "Elvis Presley: The Early Years" The Fiftiesweb, http://www.fifties web.com/elvis.htm.
2. James L. Dickerson, *Colonel Tom Parker: The Curious Life of Elvis Presley's Eccentric Manager* (Cooper Square Press, 2001), http://www.popmatters.com/books/reviews/c/colonel-tomparker.shtml.
3. *Time,* March 6, 1978, cover.
4. Dan Pages, "UCLA Researchers Offer First Scientific Evidence Showing Sports Figures As Positive Influences in Lives of Teen Admirers." The Regents of the University of California, http://www.ph.ucla.edu/pr/news item012802.html.
5. Ibid.
6. For more information about Tonya Ruiz, go to: http://www.beauty-quest.net/.
7. *Britney and Kevin: Chaotic,* UPN, May 17, 2005.
8. Justin, e-mail message to authors, July 20, 2005.
9. Information was gathered from "R. Kelly," http://www.rotten.com/library/bio/entertainers/music/r-kelly/.
10. "R. Kelly," Owner: America Online, Inc., http://music.channel.aol.com/artist/main.adp?tab=bio&artistid=45175.
11. James Sang Li, e-mail to authors, July 29, 2005.
12. Suzanne Eller, *Real Issues, Real Teens: What Every Parent Needs to Know*, (Colorado Springs: Cook Communications, 2004).

CHAPTER 3
SEX, LIES, AND FASHION

1. Kevin McCullough, "Abercrombie & Fitch to Your Kids: Group Sex Now!" WorldNetDaily.com, http://www.wnd.com/news/article.asp?ARTICLE_ID=35579.
2. "Clothier Pushes Porn, Group Sex to Youths," WorldNetDaily.com, http://www.wnd.com/news/article.asp?ARTICLE_ID=35604.
3. Author's Note: *Buck Fuddy* is a takeoff on the term *F**k Buddy,* a term used to indicate a friend (buddy) you have sex with but are otherwise not committed to.
4. "20 Questions With Ned Vizzini," About, Inc., http://teenadvice.about.com/library/books/blNedVizzini110.htm.

5. Danna Gresh, *And the Bride Wore White* and *Secret Keeper: The Delicate Power of Modesty* (Chicago: Moody Publishers, 2000 and 2002, respectively).

6. Bob Gresh, *Who Moved the Goalpost?* (Chicago: Moody Publishers, 2001).

7. Dannah Gresh, "The Fashion Battle: Is It Worth Fighting?" Life and Liberty Ministries, http://www.lifeandlibertyministries.com/archives/000204.php.

8. "Media and Girls," Media Awareness Network, http://www.media-awareness.ca/english/issues/stereotyping/ women_and_girls/women_girls.cfm.

9. From the Doxology.

10. Allison Bottke, *A Stitch in Time: Confessions of a Plastic Surgery Junkie* (Minneapolis: Bethany House Publishers, 2006).

CHAPTER 4
SEX, LIES, AND SPRING BREAK

1. "Media and Girls," Fusionanomaly, http://fusionanomaly.net/dionysus.html.

2. Ibid.

3. "Spring Break History—cont'd," Tripsmarter.com, http://www.tripsmarter.com/panamacity/springbreak/sb_history2.htm.

4. Actor, recently seen in *The Dukes of Hazzard* (Warner Brothers, 2005).

5. *Spring Break's Most Outrageous Moments,* MTV, 2005.

6. Carleton Kendrick, "Spring Break: What Parents Need to Know," Family Education, http://life.familyeducation.com/work-and-college/drugs-and-alcohol/ 36557.html.

7. Dawn Henthorn, "Spring Break Safety," About, Inc., http://goflorida.about.com/od/planningyourtrip/a/ springbrksafety.htm.

8. Ibid.

9. http://www.usatoday.com/life/lifestyle/2005-03-30-spring-break_x.htm.

10. "Information on Mexico: Spring Break in Mexico," Embassy of the United States, http://mexico.usembassy.gov/mexico/eacs_spring_ break.html.

11. Ibid.

12. "Daytona Beach 2006 Spring Break Guide," About, Inc., http://goflorida.about.com/ od/daytonaeastcoast/ss/ springbreak_db_9.htm.

13. "Spring Break History," Tourist Network Interactive, http://www.tripsmarter.com/panamacity/springbreak/sb_history.htm.

CHAPTER 5
SEX, LIES, AND THE PROM

1. Janet Holm McHenry, *Prayer Changes Teens: How to Parent from Your Knees* (Colorado Springs: WaterBrook, 2003), 112.
2. After eleven years of decline in the number of high school seniors reporting daily drinking, the numbers increased 16 percent proportionally from 2.5 percent in 1993 to 2.9 percent in 2000. However, from 1999 to 2000 there was a 15 percent decrease in the proportion of high school seniors reporting daily drinking. "Fast Facts About Underage Drinking." Owner: The Century Council, 1310 G Street, NW, Suite 600, Washington DC, http://www.centurycouncil.org/underage/fastfacts1.html.
3. Janet Holm McHenry, e-mail message to authors, August 16, 2005.
4. Greg Behrendt and Liz Tuccillo, *He's Just Not That Into You* (New York: Simon Spotlight Entertainment, 2004).

CHAPTER 6
SEX, LIES, AND DATING 101

1. Eva Marie Everson and Jessica Everson, *Sex, Lies, and the Media* (Colorado Spring: Life Journey, Cook Communications, 2005), 112.
2. Jill Savage and Pam Farrel, *Got Teens? Time-Tested Answers for Moms of Teens and Tweens* (Eugene, OR: Harvest House, 2005), 71.
3. Said to author in a direct conversation.
4. Stormie Omartian, *The Power of a Praying Parent,* (Eugene, OR: Harvest House Publishers, July 1995).
5. Sources include RAINN, University of South Florida, Federal Bureau of Investigation (Uniform Crime Statistics, 1996), U.S. Department of Justice, Violence against Women (Bureau of Justice Statistics, U.S. Dept. of Justice, 1994), http://womensissues.about.com/od/rapecrisis/a/rapestats.htm
6. "Date Rape: What You Should Know." The Nemours Foundation, http://kidshealth.org/teen/your_mind/problems/ date_rape.html.
7. Clark Staten, "'Roofies', The New 'Date Rape' Drug of Choice," Emergency Net News, http://www.emergency.com/roofies.htm.
8. Push and Mireille Silcott, *A Rough Guide to Ecstacy,* reproduced with permission from *The Book of E* (London: Omnibus Press, 2000), www./urban75.com/Drugs/e_guide.html.
9. "GHB," urban75, http://www.urban75.com/Drugs/gbh.html.
10. G. W. (Bill) Reynolds III, *Sin City* (Jacksonville, FL: River City Press, 2003). A school principal, telephone conversation with authors.

11. Judith Reisman, "Raped in Class," WorldNetDaily, http://www.world-netdaily.com/news/article.asp?ARTICLE_ID=24096.

Chapter 7
Sex, Lies, STDs, and Pregnancy

1. *Sex and America's Teenagers*, (New York: AGI, 1994), 19–20. http://www.iwannaknow.org/.
2. http://kidshealth.org/teen/sexual_health/stds/std.html.
3. "Sexually Transmitted Diseases," National Physicians Center, http://www.physicianscenter.org/content_page8.asp.
4. P. Donovan, *Testing Positive: Sexually Transmitted Disease and the Public Health Response* (New York: AGI, 1993) 24, http://www.iwannaknow.org/.
5. Ibid.
6. Ibid.
7. Jennifer M. Parker, "The Sex Lives of Christian Teens," *Today's Christian,* March/April 2003. Christianity Today International, http://www.christianitytoday.com/tc/2003/002/7.28.html.
8. "Sexually Transmitted Diseases," National Physicians Center, http://www.physicianscenter.org/content_page8.asp.
9. Thomas R. Eng and William T. Butler, eds., *The Hidden Epidemic— Confronting Sexually Transmitted Disease Institute of Medicine* (Washington, DC: National Academy Press, 1997).
10. Centers for Disease Control and Prevention. (September 1998). Summary of Notifiable Disease, United States 1997. Morbidity and Mortality Weekly Report 46 (54).
11. "Clamydia," National Institute of Allergy and Infectious Diseases, http://www.mydna.com/health/sexual/chlamydia/; http://www.niaid.nih.gov/factsheets/stdclam.htm.
12. "Clamydia," myDNA.com, http://www.mydna.com/health/sexual/chlamydia/.
13. Miranda Hitti, *Chlamydia Most Common in Teens, Young Adults (WebMD Medical News),* July 13, 2005, http://aolsvc.health. webmd. aol.com/content/article/108/109012.htm?src=AOLConditionWidget.
14. "Treatment of Gonorrhea," myDNA.com, http://www.mydna.com/health/sexual/gonorrhea/overview/treat.html; "Gonorrhea," myDNA.com, National Institute of Allergy and Infectious Diseases, http://www.niaid. nih.gov/factsheets/stdgon.htm; "Gonorrhea," Wikipedia, http://en.wiki pedia.org/wiki/Gonorrhea.

15. "Gonorrhea," The Nemours Foundation, http://kidshealth.org/teen/sexual_health/stds/std_gonorrhea.html.

16. L. Westrom, "Incidence, Prevalence, and Trends of Acute Pelvic Inflammatory Disease and Its Consequences in Industrialized Countries," *American Journal of Obstetrics and Gynecology* 138 (1980): 880–92.

17. "HIV Infection and AIDS: An Overview," National Institute of Allergy and Infectious Diseases, http://www.niaid.nih.gov/factsheets/hivinf.htm; "AIDS, Sex, & Teens," Avert.org, http://www.avert.org/young.htm; "AIDS/HIV," myDNA.com, http://www.mydna.com/health/sexual/aids/; (WebMD Corporation). aolsvc.health.webmd.aol.com/home.default.

18. "Introduction to HIV Infection." Owner: myDNA.com http://www.mydna.com/health/sexual/aids/overview/aidsoverview.html.

19. Ibid.

20. "AIDS, Sex, & Teens," Avert.org, http://www.avert.org/young.htm.

21. "Syphillis," University of Missouri-Rolla Student Health Services, http://campus.umr.edu/studenthealth/sexual_ health/syphillis.html. "Syphilis," National Institute of Allergy and Infectious Diseases, http://www.niaid.nih.gov/factsheets/std syph.htm. "Syphillis," Teens for Teens, http://www.teensforteens.net/sexuality/ std/s/syphillis.html.

22. "Syphillis," University of Missouri-Rolla Student Health Services, http://campus.umr.edu/studenthealth/sexual_ health/syphillis.html.

23. Information for "Other STDs" from "Pelvic Inflammatory Diesase," Arboris Limited, http://www.medinfo.co.uk/ conditions/pid.html. "Gonorrhea," National Institute of Allergy and Infectious Diseases, http://www.niaid.nih.gov/ factsheets/stdgon.htm. "Understanding Genital Herpes," Novartis Pharmaceuticals Corporation, http://www.famvir.com/info/simplystated/what_is_genital_herpes.jsp. "Herpes Information," The Complete Herpes Information Center, http://www.globalherbalsupplies.com/ herpes/ about.html. "Genital Warts," Department of Public Health, City and County of San Francisco, http://www.dph.sf.ca.us/HealthInfo/std_warts.htm. "Genital Warts," Centers for Disease Control, http://www.cdc.gov/std/stats/tables/table47.htm.

24. D. T. Fleming, et al. "Herpes Simplex Virus type 2 in the United States, 1976 to 1994," *New England Journal of Medicine* 337 (1997): 1105–11.

25. "Herpes Information," The Complete Herpes Information Center, http://www.globalherbalsupplies.com/herpes/stats.html.

26. Ibid., http://www.globalherbalsupplies.com/herpes/about.html.

27. Ibid.

28. Julie K. Endersbe, *Teen Fathers*, (Mankato, MN: Capstone Press, 2000), 42.
29. Julie K. Endersbe, *Teen Pregnancy: Tough Choices* (Mankato, MN: Capstone Press, 2000), 6.
30. Endersbe, *Teen Fathers*, 9.
31. Endersbe, *Teen Pregnancy*, 4.
32. Linda Rooks, "Why Not Adoption?" *Focus on the Family* magazine, http://www.family.org/fofmag/sl/a0024069.cfm.
33. Tricia Goyer, *Life Interrupted: The Scoop on Being a Young Mom*, (Grand Rapids: Zondervan, 2004).
34. Ibid.

CHAPTER 8
SEX, LIES, AND ABSTINENCE

1. "QuickStats: Percentage of Never-Married Teens Aged 15–19 Years Who Reported Ever Having Sexual Intercourse, by Sex and by Age Group—United States, 1995–2002," MMWR Weekly, http://www.cdc.gov/mmwr/preview/mmwrhtml/ mm5430a7.htm.
2. J. C. Abma, et. al., "Teenagers in the United States: sexual activity, contraceptive use, and childbearing, 2002," Vital Health Stat 23(24), 2004, http://www.cdc.gov/nchs/data/series/sr_23/sr23_024.pdf.
3. Eva Marie Everson and Jessica Everson, *Sex, Lies, and the Media* (Colorado Springs: Life Journey, Cook Communications, 2005), 218–19.
4. For more information about this project, including how to start one in your community, go to: www.thinksmartflorida.com.

CHAPTER 9
SEX, LIES, AND THE REST OF THEIR LIVES

1. While we certainly don't want to encourage our teens to marry their cousins, the focus here should be on not being unequally yoked.
2. The focus here will be that a marriage blessed by God is indeed richly blessed by God.

Chapter 10
Hope and Help for Parents of Today's High School Students

1. *I Can Do Bad All By Myself,* directed by Tyler Perry (New York: Lion's Gate, 2005).

Additional copies of *Sex, Lies, and High School*
and other Life Journey titles are available
wherever good books are sold.

If you have enjoyed this book,
or if it has had an impact on your life,
we would like to hear from you.

Please contact us at:

LIFE JOURNEY BOOKS
Cook Communications Ministries, Dept. 201
4050 Lee Vance View
Colorado Springs, CO 80918

Or visit our Web site:
www.cookministries.com

LIFE JOURNEY®
Bringing Home the Message for Life